KIDS IN CRISIS

Allison T Garrett

CONTENTS

INTRODUCTION

Trauma Isn't the Whole Story

As a kid growing up in the 70s, I didn't have time to worry about anxiety or mental health days. In fact, "trauma" wasn't even a word that entered our vocabulary. I was part of the Generation X crew, a generation known for its independence, grit, and toughness. We were the latchkey kids, the ones who drank from the hose, rode bikes without helmets, and navigated life without our parents hovering. We played outside until the streetlights came on, walked to the corner store alone, and figured things out for ourselves when things went sideways.

That was life back then. We weren't shielded from challenges, and because of that, we learned resilience. But I didn't realize just how much I would need that resilience until one pivotal moment in my life.

I was 13 when my world changed forever. My mother died suddenly, leaving me and my siblings in a whirlwind of grief and confusion. I dropped out of 8th grade—not because I didn't value school, but because I had to step up. I became a caretaker, thrust into a role far beyond my years. My father, overwhelmed with the sudden loss, relied on me to help with my younger siblings. So, I did what I had to do.

I was the one taking the bus to the bank to help manage what little money we had. I skated to the laundromat on roller skates—because why not multitask, right? I shopped for clothes on Jamaica Avenue and pressed my siblings' hair with a hot comb, determined to keep some normalcy in our lives. I didn't think of these things as extraordinary; they were just what had to be done. I learned how to navigate the world, fix problems, and keep going.

Two years later, my father passed away. I was 15, and suddenly, I had no parents. I had already been forced to grow up fast, but now there was no one left to guide me. At that moment, I could have crumbled under the weight of loss and responsibility. And yet, I didn't. I didn't have the luxury to give up. I had already learned so much about resilience before my father passed—now it was just time to apply it.

What I've realized over the years is that this wasn't trauma that defined me, nor was it the loss of my parents that shaped my future. It was the resilience that had been instilled in me long before that final blow. It was the everyday struggles, the tough love, the figuring-it-out-on-my-own moments that truly molded me.

Today, I look at the world around me, and I see a generation of kids—and adults—who are drowning in talk of trauma. We've become obsessed with mental health labels, excuses, and the idea that every hardship is something to be protected from. But here's the thing: trauma isn't the end of the story, and it's certainly not the whole story. Resilience is.

Yes, there's pain, there's hardship, and there's loss. But there's also strength, perseverance, and the ability to overcome. I'm not saying that trauma doesn't matter, or that mental health isn't important—it is. But what I am saying is that we've forgotten the other side of the coin. We've forgotten how to teach our kids, and ourselves, how to bounce back, how to problem-solve, how to take the bus in the rain with two kids instead of calling out of work. We've forgotten that resilience is not just an option, it's a necessity.

This book is about that necessity. It is about raising kids who can handle life's challenges—not by avoiding them, but by learning how to face them head-on. It's about teaching ourselves how to build the kind of inner strength that turns adversity into an advantage.

We're going to explore a world where trauma isn't a stopping point, but a launching pad. A world where kids, and adults, can grow, thrive, and succeed—not despite the challenges they face, but because of them. This isn't just about surviving, it's about thriving through resilience.

CHAPTER ONE

The Resilience Deficit

Let's get real about this epidemic. The resilience deficit is real, and we're seeing its effects in how kids and adults alike handle setbacks. Gone are the days of grit and determination as primary values. Now, it's all about avoiding discomfort.

When I was growing up, we didn't have fancy terms for every little bump in the road. We just dealt with it. Our car broke down? We walked or took the bus. Our parents didn't coddle us, and they certainly didn't shelter us from every little inconvenience. Today, things are different. Society seems obsessed with insulating kids from failure or struggle, and it's robbing them of one of the most critical life skills: resilience.

The Great Grit Decline

Take a moment to think about how you handle problems in your life. Are you someone who looks for a way out or a way through? The answer might say more about your upbringing than you realize. For generations, resilience—also known as grit, perseverance, or plain old toughness—was instilled in us. We were expected to solve problems, make do with what we had, and figure things out on our own.

As kids in the '70s and '80s, we had no choice but to develop resilience. We didn't have cell phones to text our parents when things went wrong. When my mom passed away and I had to step up for my family, there was no time for self-pity or expecting someone to swoop in and save the day. We had to keep moving. But here's the thing—this wasn't a special experience. Most of us were growing up like that. That was normal. Resilience wasn't an option; it was a requirement for survival.

Today, however, we're seeing what I call the "Great Grit Decline." Children are shielded from adversity by well-meaning adults who are afraid of letting them fail. Instead of developing problem-solving skills, kids are conditioned to believe that if things don't go their way, someone else will fix it. This mindset follows them into adulthood, leaving them unprepared for life's inevitable challenges.

Why Are We Afraid of Discomfort?

In our world today, comfort is king. Parents are doing everything they can to make sure their children are always safe, always happy, and always comfortable. From bubble-wrapping kids on the playground to calling teachers at the first sign of a bad grade, the message we're sending is that discomfort is to be avoided at all costs. But here's the reality: Discomfort is a part of life. It's unavoidable, and more importantly, it's necessary for growth.

When we shield kids from discomfort, we're doing them a huge disservice. We're telling them that life should always be easy, and when it's not, they won't know how to handle it. Imagine a kid who's never been allowed to struggle in school—what happens when they face real academic challenges? Instead of learning to problem-solve, they crumble under the pressure because they were never given the tools to push through tough situations.

As adults, we can see this play out in the workplace. I've seen employees cancel job interviews because they couldn't find the location or call out of work because of a mild headache. These are people who were never taught that sometimes, you just have to push through the tough times. They weren't raised with the expectation that life isn't always going to be convenient or easy.

The Science of Resilience

Let's get scientific for a minute. Resilience isn't just a feel-good idea; it's a real, measurable trait. Studies show that resilience has a biological foundation. There's this thing called neuroplasticity, which means that our brains are constantly changing and adapting based on our experiences. The more adversity we face, the more our brains adapt to handle future stress.

Dr. Michael Ungar, a resilience researcher, talks about how children who experience manageable stress and challenges grow up to be more resilient adults. They develop what he calls "toughness circuits" in their brains. These circuits help them bounce back faster when things go wrong. But here's the kicker—if kids aren't exposed to stress or adversity, those circuits don't develop properly.

Think about it this way: When you exercise, you break down your muscles so they can rebuild stronger. The same principle applies to resilience. If kids never experience emotional or mental challenges, they don't build up the resilience muscle. They become fragile, like glass, easily shattered by even the smallest setback.

Real Talk: Helicopter Parenting and the Bubble Wrap Generation

Let's talk about the elephant in the room: helicopter parenting. You've heard of it. You've probably even seen it in action. Helicopter parents are those who hover over their kids, making sure every little thing goes perfectly. They intervene in every aspect of their children's lives, from playground spats to school projects. But here's the harsh truth: Helicopter parenting isn't helping anyone. It's creating a generation of kids who are completely ill-equipped to handle life on their own.

I once saw a parent complete their child's science fair project for them because the kid was struggling. What kind of message does that send? It tells the child that they can't do hard things, and that someone else will always step in when things get tough. But life doesn't work that way.

In my generation, parents didn't hover. They didn't swoop in to fix everything. We were allowed to fail, and we learned from those failures. If you forgot your lunch, you went hungry. If you fell off your bike, you got up, dusted yourself off, and tried again. That's how resilience is built—through struggle, failure, and learning to get back up.

Embrace the Messy

Alright, enough of the doom and gloom. There's good news here. We can turn this around! The resilience deficit isn't irreversible. We just need to start allowing kids—and ourselves—to embrace the messiness of life. Failure isn't something to be feared; it's something to be learned from.

Let's start by letting kids solve their own problems. If your child comes home complaining about a tough situation at school, resist the urge to step in and fix it. Instead, ask them how they think they should handle it. Give them the chance to figure things out on their own. Will it always go perfectly? Nope. But that's the point! They need to learn that not everything goes according to plan, and that's okay.

Another fun idea? Stop over-scheduling. Kids need downtime. They need unstructured play to learn how to navigate the world without constant guidance. When we let them play without an agenda, we give them the space to develop critical problem-solving skills. They learn how to negotiate, how to compromise, and how to handle disappointment when things don't go their way.

Building Resilience in Adults

Now, I know what you're thinking—what about us adults? We've grown up, and maybe we missed out on building some of that resilience ourselves. Don't worry, it's never too late! Building resilience as an adult is possible, and it's crucial for thriving in today's world.

Start by getting comfortable with discomfort. Try pushing yourself out of your comfort zone regularly. Whether it's taking on a new challenge at work, trying something new in your personal life, or simply facing a fear, each time you do, you're building your resilience muscle.

And remember, resilience doesn't mean you won't feel stressed or anxious. It means you know how to keep going even when you do. It's about bouncing back, not never falling down.

Wrapping It Up: The Future of Resilience

In a world that's constantly changing and often unpredictable, resilience is more important than ever. We need to stop bubble-wrapping our kids and ourselves and start embracing the idea that failure and discomfort are part of life. The resilience deficit is real, but so is our ability to turn it around.

By allowing ourselves and our kids to experience adversity, we'll all be better equipped to handle the inevitable challenges that life throws our way. So, let's roll up our sleeves, dust ourselves off, and get to work. Because life isn't about avoiding the storms—it's about learning how to dance in the rain.

CHAPTER TWO

When Did We Become So Fragile?

Remember when the idea of 'tough love' was about preparing kids for the real world? We were taught that life wasn't always fair, and that grit and determination would help us navigate those inevitable bumps in the road. But now, fragility seems to be in vogue. From schools to social environments, we've somehow decided that shielding our children from any form of adversity is the way to go. It's like the pendulum has swung too far, and instead of preparing kids for the challenges of life, we're cushioning them from it entirely.

The Evolution from Grit to Fragility

Let's be nostalgic, back to a time when kids were expected to handle themselves. Growing up in the '70s and '80s, if you were bullied on the playground, your parents didn't immediately rush to the school demanding action. They told you to stand up for yourself. You were taught to confront challenges head-on, not run away from them. This wasn't seen as neglectful or uncaring; it was viewed as a necessary part of growing up.

So, what happened? How did we go from "figure it out" to "let me fix it for you"? It seems somewhere along the way, we collectively decided that our kids should never experience discomfort. But in doing so, we've robbed them of the resilience that's forged in the fires of adversity.

A big part of this shift stems from a cultural fear of failure. It's no longer okay for kids to fall down and scrape their knees—physically or metaphorically. Instead, we've become obsessed with making sure they never fall in the first place. Helicopter parenting, safe spaces, and participation trophies are all symptoms of this larger problem: we've become so focused on protecting our children that we've forgotten how important it is to let them stumble, fall, and get back up again.

The Cost of Overprotection

But here's the kicker—this overprotection has a cost. When kids aren't allowed to experience failure or adversity, they don't learn how to deal with it. They become fragile. We've all seen it: young adults who crumble at the slightest sign of challenge or discomfort. They're ill-equipped to handle rejection, failure, or even mild criticism. Instead of developing coping skills, they've learned to avoid discomfort at all costs.

This isn't just anecdotal; studies back it up. According to research, kids who are shielded from challenges are more likely to experience anxiety, depression, and a sense of helplessness as they grow older. Dr. Jonathan Haidt, a social psychologist, refers to this as "safetyism," a mindset where avoiding harm becomes the goal. But in doing so, we're inadvertently creating a generation of fragile individuals who lack the ability to cope with life's inevitable difficulties.

Fragility in the Classroom

Let's look at our schools for a moment. They've become ground zero for this fragility epidemic. Once, schools were where we learned not just academics but life lessons. We faced challenges, navigated social hierarchies, and dealt with the consequences of our actions. But today's schools have adopted a "no fail" mentality. Kids are passed through the system even if they haven't mastered the material. Teachers are discouraged from giving harsh feedback for fear of hurting a student's self-esteem. And when conflict arises, it's often handled with kid gloves, with administrators stepping in before students have a chance to work things out themselves.

Take the rise of trigger warnings and safe spaces as another example. While well-intentioned, these measures can sometimes send the message that students are too fragile to handle difficult topics or uncomfortable situations. Instead of teaching students how to think critically and engage with challenging ideas, we're teaching them to avoid anything that might make them uncomfortable. But life doesn't come with trigger warnings, and by shielding students from discomfort, we're setting them up for failure when they inevitably face it in the real world.

The Fragility Epidemic in Adulthood

The problem doesn't stop when kids grow up. We're seeing this fragility spill over into adulthood, too. In the workplace, more and more employees are struggling to handle even minor setbacks. When things don't go their way, they're quick to disengage or give up altogether. This is the result of a culture that's raised people to expect constant validation and smooth sailing, rather than preparing them for the inevitable ups and downs of life.

In recent years, we've seen the rise of "cancel culture" and public outrage at even the slightest misstep. This is fragility at its finest—an inability to cope with differing opinions, criticism, or challenges to our worldview. Instead of engaging in healthy debate or learning from our mistakes, we've created a culture that punishes people for being imperfect. It's as if we've lost the ability to navigate conflict in a mature and productive way.

Real Talk: Tough Love vs. Coddling

Let's be honest—no one likes to see their kids struggle. It's hard to watch someone you love go through pain or hardship. But tough love isn't about being cruel or indifferent; it's about teaching kids to be self-reliant. The world isn't going to coddle them, and as parents, educators, and adults, we do them a disservice by trying to shield them from every uncomfortable situation.

I remember a time when I was about 10 years old, trying to get my roller skates on without help. I struggled for what felt like hours, frustrated and angry that my parents wouldn't just do it for me. But you know what? I eventually figured it out. And that feeling of accomplishment—of having solved the problem on my own—was worth all the frustration.

That's what we need to remember: kids need to face challenges and solve problems on their own. They need to feel the satisfaction of overcoming adversity. It's not about letting them flounder without guidance; it's about giving them the tools to navigate tough situations and then stepping back to let them use those tools.

Raising Stronger Kids

So, how do we fix this? How do we start raising kids who are more resilient and less fragile? Here's the fun part—it's not as complicated as we might think. The key is to start small, introducing manageable challenges and letting kids learn how to navigate them.

1. **Stop solving all their problems**: When your child comes to you with an issue, resist the urge to fix it right away. Instead, ask them what they think they should do. Encourage them to brainstorm solutions and then let them try out their ideas. Will it always work? Nope. But that's the point. They need to learn how to handle failure and bounce back.

2. **Introduce a little bit of discomfort**: This one's simple—let kids get bored, frustrated, or uncomfortable from time to time. It's okay if they don't get what they want immediately. Learning to tolerate discomfort is a critical life skill, and the earlier they start, the better.

3. **Teach them to fail gracefully**: This one's a game-changer. Instead of shielding kids from failure, teach them how to fail with grace. Let them know that failure isn't the end of the world—it's just part of the process. When they fail, encourage them to reflect on what they learned and how they can improve next time.

4. **Model resilience**: Kids learn by watching the adults in their lives. If we show them that we can handle setbacks and challenges with grace and determination, they'll be more likely to do the same. Let them see you face adversity and come out the other side stronger.

Building Resilience in Ourselves

Of course, we can't teach kids to be resilient if we're fragile ourselves. So, it's important for adults to work on building their own resilience. Life throws curveballs at all of us, but how we respond to those challenges sets the tone for the next generation.

Start by embracing failure in your own life. Take risks, step outside your comfort zone, and allow yourself to learn from your mistakes. When you model resilience, you're not just benefiting yourself—you're showing your children, your coworkers, and the people around you that it's okay to struggle. It's okay to fail. What matters is how you pick yourself up and keep going.

Wrapping It Up: From Fragile to Strong

The fragility epidemic is real, but it's not irreversible. By letting kids—and ourselves—experience adversity, failure, and discomfort, we can start to rebuild the resilience that's been lost. It's time to stop coddling and start challenging. Because in the end, life isn't about avoiding difficulty; it's about developing the strength to face it head-on.

CHAPTER THREE

Helicopter Parenting and the Fragile Generation

Helicopter parenting has become so commonplace that we've almost normalized it. But what happens when we hover too much over our kids, micromanaging every aspect of their lives? We create a generation that can't fend for itself, a generation that struggles with basic life skills and crumbles under pressure. Helicopter parenting isn't just an overprotective style—it's producing real consequences, ones that we see playing out across homes, schools, and workplaces.

The Rise of Helicopter Parenting

Before we dive into the damage, let's take a step back and look at how we got here. Helicopter parenting, as the term suggests, is the tendency of parents to "hover" over their children, managing their every move. It's born out of love, of course. We want our kids to succeed, avoid pain, and be happy. But somewhere along the line, this protective instinct has spiraled into something far more controlling.

Parents have become hyper-involved in every decision their child makes; from what they wear in the morning to which extracurriculars they take after school. And it's not just during childhood—helicopter parents are known to follow their kids into adulthood, often guiding their choices in college and even interfering in their work lives.

How did we go from sending kids outside to play until the streetlights came on to tracking their every move on a GPS app? Some of it stems from the heightened fears about safety—stories of kidnappings, bullying, and school shootings have left parents feeling like they can't let their guard down for a second. Add to that the pressures of competitive academic environments, and you've got a recipe for parents stepping in to solve every little problem, big or small.

Micromanagement: The Death of Independence

At first glance, helicopter parenting may seem like a natural extension of caring for your child, but when you get into the details, you see how harmful it can be. When parents micromanage every aspect of their child's life, children miss out on learning key life skills. Think about the basic things you learned just by being allowed to figure things out on your own—how to solve a disagreement with a friend, how to budget your allowance, or even how to manage time when juggling multiple responsibilities.

If parents do all the heavy lifting—calling teachers, fixing schedules, planning every step forward—kids never learn how to do those things for themselves. And here's the reality: one day, those kids are going to have to make decisions without a safety net. But without the practice, they're likely to freeze under pressure or make poor choices because they never got the chance to learn from small mistakes.

Imagine you're 19 years old, away at college for the first time, and you realize you don't know how to do laundry. Your mom always did it for you. Do you call her? Or maybe you've got a big project due at work, and you're overwhelmed because no one's around to remind you to break it down into manageable tasks. This is what we're seeing with young adults today—without the necessary life skills, they feel lost when they finally step into the world.

The Fragile Generation

Helicopter parenting is creating what many are now calling "the fragile generation." This isn't just hyperbole; psychologists and educators are raising the alarm about how ill-prepared young people are for real-life challenges. When parents shield their children from every discomfort, they inadvertently send the message that their child isn't capable of handling things on their own. This fosters a sense of dependency and fragility.

Dr. Peter Gray, a psychologist and author, speaks directly to this issue, highlighting how modern parenting is producing children who are less resilient. According to his research, kids today are suffering from higher levels of anxiety and depression, largely because they aren't given the tools to handle failure, stress, or adversity. He notes, "The more children are protected from experiencing adversity, the less capable they become of dealing with it when it inevitably arises."

Life isn't always smooth sailing. It comes with challenges, heartbreaks, and setbacks. But instead of preparing our kids for those realities, helicopter parenting wraps them in bubble wrap, ensuring they never get the opportunity to build their emotional muscles. Sure, your child might not skin their knee today, but when they face a major hurdle later on—like failing an exam, losing a job, or ending a relationship—they won't have the emotional endurance to cope.

Overparenting in the Classroom

Let's shift focus for a second to see how this plays out in the educational system. Schools have long been places where kids learn not only academics but life skills—how to deal with difficult situations, manage their time, and collaborate with others. However, helicopter parenting has infiltrated the classroom too. Teachers are increasingly reporting that parents are intervening in ways they never used to—challenging grades, demanding special treatment, or even doing their children's homework for them.

What happens when parents try to control the academic process? First, it puts undue pressure on teachers, who are caught between fostering independence and satisfying parents who expect their children to be coddled. But more importantly, it prevents children from learning how to advocate for themselves. When a student doesn't agree with a grade or struggles to complete an assignment, they should be learning to approach their teacher to discuss the problem. Instead, parents are doing this work for them.

This doesn't just harm the student's learning; it undermines their confidence. How can a child believe they're capable of handling schoolwork or challenges if their parents are constantly stepping in to take over? Without the chance to struggle and ultimately succeed, these kids never build the self-assurance that comes from mastering difficult tasks.

Fragile in the Workplace

The consequences of helicopter parenting don't end when kids finish school. When this fragile generation enters the workplace, the lack of life skills and independence becomes even more pronounced. Employers are increasingly noting that young workers struggle with problem-solving, time management, and taking initiative. They're waiting for someone to tell them exactly what to do, just as their parents have done for them their entire lives.

In a workplace setting, this fragility manifests in several ways. There's the inability to handle criticism—many young employees are so accustomed to constant praise and validation that even mild constructive feedback sends them spiraling. They also have difficulty taking ownership of tasks, often expecting others to step in and do the hard work for them. This lack of resilience makes it hard for them to thrive in environments where innovation, grit, and adaptability are key.

And let's talk about helicopter parents who follow their children into adulthood—there are parents who call their adult children's bosses to complain about work schedules, low pay, or perceived unfair treatment. It's a real thing. When parents interfere at this level, they're not just embarrassing their children, they're undermining their ability to mature into self-sufficient adults.

Real Talk: Why You've Got to Stop Hovering

Okay, let's have some real talk here. As parents, our job isn't to solve all of our children's problems—it's to equip them with the tools to solve their own. That's the essence of good parenting: raising kids who can function without us. Helicopter parenting might feel like love, but it's doing more harm than good. We have to trust that our kids are capable of handling life's bumps, bruises, and setbacks. It's time to put the helicopter on the ground and give our kids the space to learn, grow, and sometimes fail.

Remember when you were young, and you had to figure things out for yourself? Maybe it was scary or uncomfortable at times, but it made you stronger. It gave you the skills to navigate adulthood with confidence. If we want our kids to develop that same strength, we need to stop hovering and start letting them take control.

Landing the Helicopter

So how do we land the helicopter? It's not about abandoning our kids or leaving them to fend for themselves in a harsh world. It's about stepping back just enough to let them figure things out. Here are a few practical tips to help:

1. **Delegate Responsibility**: Start small by giving your child age-appropriate responsibilities. Let them pack their own lunch, decide how to spend their allowance, or choose their extracurricular activities. The more decisions they

make, the more confident they'll become in their own abilities.

2. **Encourage Problem-Solving**: When your child faces a challenge, don't swoop in with the answer. Instead, ask them how they think they should handle the situation. Let them brainstorm solutions, and then support them as they put those solutions into action.

3. **Celebrate Failure**: This might sound counterintuitive, but failure is an essential part of learning. When your child makes a mistake, don't rush to fix it or soften the blow. Help them see failure as a valuable learning experience. Talk about what went wrong and how they can approach it differently next time.

4. **Set Boundaries for Involvement**: It's okay to be involved in your child's life, but there's a fine line between involvement and micromanagement. Set clear boundaries for yourself. Ask yourself, "Does my child really need me to do this, or can they handle it on their own?"

5. **Model Independence**: If you want your child to be independent, show them what that looks like. Take risks, make decisions, and handle your own setbacks with grace and resilience. Your kids are watching, and they'll learn more from what you do than what you say.

Wrapping It Up: Raising a Generation of Self-Sufficient Kids

Helicopter parenting might seem like the best way to keep our kids safe and secure, but in reality, it's leaving them unprepared for the real world. By stepping back and letting our kids handle life's challenges, we give them the chance to develop the independence, resilience, and confidence they'll need to thrive. It's time to land the helicopter and start raising a generation of self-sufficient, capable young people. They're ready for it, and deep down, so are we.

CHAPTER FOUR

Schools: Safe Spaces or Sheltered Bubbles?

Schools used to be places where children learned not only reading, writing, and arithmetic, but also essential life skills—problem-solving, resilience, social interaction, and how to navigate difficult situations. Today, that narrative has shifted, and many schools are increasingly being seen as "sheltered bubbles," where protecting students from emotional and psychological discomfort seems to take precedence over preparing them for the real world. While safe spaces are often created with the best intentions, they may inadvertently prevent students from developing the resilience they need to cope with life outside of the school walls.

The Emergence of Safe Spaces

The term "safe space" originated in marginalized communities, where it was used to describe physical and social environments where individuals could express themselves without fear of judgment, harassment, or emotional harm. In theory, creating such spaces in schools makes sense—especially when students face issues like bullying, discrimination, or trauma.

However, the concept of safe spaces has evolved over time. It's no longer just about creating environments free from violence and hatred; it's about shielding students from any form of discomfort, challenge, or adversity. In many cases, schools have implemented policies that aim to prevent students from encountering even the slightest emotional stress—whether it's controversial topics, challenging coursework, or differing opinions. And while this might sound like a good idea, it comes with unintended consequences.

Are We Protecting or Stifling Growth?

Let's get one thing straight: schools should absolutely be safe places in the sense that students shouldn't fear physical harm, extreme bullying, or emotional abuse. But when we extend the idea of safety to include protection from discomfort, we start crossing a dangerous line. The reality is that life, outside the controlled environment of school, isn't safe in this way. It's messy, unpredictable, and full of challenges. And when we overprotect students, we deny them the opportunity to build the resilience they need to navigate that reality.

By constantly protecting students from discomfort, we inadvertently send them a message that they're too fragile to handle it. We're not just protecting them from harm; we're stifling their growth. Take a look at the growing number of college students who struggle with mental health issues—many of whom cite academic pressure, failure, or social challenges as sources of distress. The spike in anxiety and depression among students suggests that, in our attempt to protect them, we may have done the opposite—we've left them ill-equipped to cope with the real world.

The Consequences of Sheltered Bubbles

The long-term consequences of sheltering students in protective bubbles can be seen in various areas of their lives. For one, students who never face adversity or conflict in school may struggle later in life when they encounter difficult situations. Imagine entering the workforce and, for the first time, having to deal with a boss who gives harsh feedback, or navigating complex personal relationships without the benefit of prior experience. If students never practice handling stress in controlled environments like school, how will they handle it in the real world, where the stakes are higher?

Another consequence is a decreased ability to tolerate differing viewpoints. Schools, once the battleground for intellectual debate and critical thinking, are increasingly becoming places where controversial topics are avoided in the name of creating emotionally safe environments. But the reality is, learning to engage with opposing perspectives is a crucial life skill. It teaches us how to negotiate, how to understand people with different worldviews, and how to grow as individuals. When we shield students from such interactions, we're not keeping them safe—we're keeping them uninformed and unprepared for a diverse world.

The Rise of Trigger Warnings and Their Impact

One of the most visible signs of this shift toward emotional protectionism in schools is the rise of trigger warnings. Originally used in therapeutic settings to alert individuals to potentially distressing content, trigger warnings have now made their way into classrooms and curricula. Professors and teachers are often expected to preface any material that could cause emotional discomfort with a trigger warning, giving students the option to opt out of engaging with it.

While the intention is to protect students with trauma, the broad use of trigger warnings has sparked debate about whether we're helping or hurting students by allowing them to avoid difficult material. After all, life doesn't come with trigger warnings. By encouraging students to sidestep any content that might make them uncomfortable, we limit their exposure to the complexity of human experience.

More importantly, avoiding discomfort doesn't build resilience—it does the opposite. Students need to learn how to confront difficult emotions and thoughts, not run from them. Resilience isn't built by avoiding challenges but by facing them head-on, processing emotions, and learning to move forward despite discomfort.

The Impact on Learning and Growth

Let's not forget the ultimate purpose of education: to prepare students for the challenges of adulthood. When schools prioritize emotional safety over intellectual rigor, students miss out on critical opportunities for learning and growth. Consider this: every significant moment of personal growth is uncomfortable. Whether it's learning how to solve a complex math problem, navigating a friendship conflict, or grappling with historical events that challenge your worldview—growth comes from being stretched, not sheltered.

Yet, more and more, we're seeing schools prioritize student comfort over challenge. Difficult books are being removed from reading lists, controversial topics are being avoided in discussions, and students are being allowed to opt out of difficult assignments. The message is clear: if it makes you uncomfortable, you don't have to engage with it. But this is not how life works. In the real world, we don't have the option to avoid every uncomfortable situation.

When we limit the types of experiences and challenges students are exposed to, we narrow their potential for growth. Intellectual growth requires encountering complex ideas, even if they challenge your current beliefs. Emotional growth requires facing and processing difficult feelings, even if they make you uncomfortable. By prioritizing safety and comfort over these forms of growth, we risk creating a generation that is intellectually shallow and emotionally fragile.

Preparing Students for the Real World

The question we need to ask is: What kind of adults do we want to raise? If the goal is to prepare young people to be resilient, capable, and adaptable, then we need to reconsider our approach to creating "safe spaces." Instead of focusing on emotional protection, we should be focusing on resilience-building. Schools should be environments where students are encouraged to engage with difficult topics, where they learn to navigate conflict, and where they develop the emotional stamina to deal with setbacks and failures.

This doesn't mean we should ignore issues like mental health or trauma. On the contrary, we should be equipping students with the tools to cope with these challenges, rather than shielding them from every potential source of discomfort. Teaching resilience means giving students strategies to manage their emotions, confront difficulties, and come out stronger on the other side.

Resilience-Building in Schools

If we want schools to be places that foster resilience rather than fragility, we need to shift the focus from protection to empowerment. Here are a few ways schools can foster resilience in students:

1. **Encourage Critical Thinking and Debate**: Instead of avoiding controversial topics, schools should encourage students to engage in thoughtful debate. This teaches them how to handle opposing viewpoints and builds the intellectual resilience needed to navigate a complex world.
2. **Allow for Failure**: Schools should embrace the idea that failure is part of the learning process. Instead of shielding students from failure, teachers can help students see failure as an opportunity to learn and grow. This fosters resilience and reduces fear of making mistakes.
3. **Teach Emotional Regulation**: Rather than avoiding difficult emotions, schools should teach students how to manage

and process them. Techniques like mindfulness, emotional literacy, and stress management can help students build the emotional resilience needed to face challenges head-on.

4. **Provide Opportunities for Real-World Problem Solving**: Schools can create opportunities for students to engage with real-world problems, whether through project-based learning, internships, or community service. These experiences teach students how to apply their knowledge in practical ways and help them develop the resilience to solve complex challenges.

5. **Promote Open Dialogue**: Schools should foster environments where students feel safe to express their thoughts and feelings, but also where they are encouraged to listen to and engage with different perspectives. This builds emotional intelligence and prepares students for life in a diverse world.

Wrapping it Up: From Sheltered Bubbles to Resilient Spaces

While the concept of safe spaces in schools started with good intentions, it has morphed into a practice that, in many cases, limits growth and resilience. If we want to prepare students for the real world, we need to create environments that challenge them intellectually and emotionally, rather than sheltering them from every discomfort. By focusing on resilience-building, schools can become places where students learn how to thrive in the face of adversity, preparing them for the complex, unpredictable world that awaits them.

CHAPTER FIVE

Social Media vs. Spirituality: Filling the Void

We live in a world where everything is instant. Instant communication, instant likes, instant gratification. At the center of this culture shift is social media, which has not only altered the way we communicate but has also profoundly changed the way we view ourselves and the world around us. For many children and teens, social media has become a kind of substitute for deeper, more meaningful practices, particularly spirituality. It's become the go-to source for validation, approval, and connection. But here's the rub—despite being more connected than ever, many young people feel more isolated, anxious, and unfulfilled.

Why? Because social media, while it may scratch the surface of our desire for connection, doesn't feed the soul. It's a shallow pool to dive into when what we need is a deep well. Spirituality, which traditionally provided a sense of purpose, belonging, and peace, has taken a backseat, leaving an emotional and spiritual void that no number of likes, comments, or followers can fill.

The Age of Validation

Let's face it—our society is obsessed with validation. From the perfectly curated Instagram photos to the viral TikTok dances, everyone's looking for approval. And that approval often comes in the form of likes, shares, and comments. For many teens and young adults, their self-worth is tied up in how their online presence is perceived. If a post doesn't perform well, it's not just a failed attempt at garnering attention—it's a reflection of their value.

And who can blame them? Social media platforms are designed to keep us hooked, giving us quick hits of dopamine every time we get a notification. It's addictive. But the problem is, it's also hollow. The validation we receive online is fleeting, and as soon as it fades, we're left with the same feelings of inadequacy that led us to seek that validation in the first place.

This constant need for approval creates a vicious cycle of external validation-seeking behavior, which pulls us further away from looking inward. Spirituality, on the other hand, is about finding peace and meaning from within. It's about understanding that our value doesn't come from what others think of us but from something deeper, something unshakeable.

The Spiritual Void

As social media has risen, spirituality—whether it be organized religion, meditation, mindfulness, or simply a connection to something greater than oneself—has declined. For centuries, spirituality provided a foundation for understanding our place in the world. It offered answers to life's big questions: Why are we here? What is our purpose? How do we find inner peace?

But in today's hyper-connected world, these questions are often drowned out by the noise of social media. We're too busy scrolling, liking, and posting to take a moment to reflect on what really matters. And the result? A deep sense of emptiness.

There's something about social media that amplifies this feeling. It's a space that constantly reminds us that we're not enough—that we don't have enough followers, enough likes, enough attention. When young people see their peers living what seems to be perfect lives, it reinforces the idea that their own life is somehow lacking. This comparison trap can be emotionally devastating, leading to anxiety, depression, and a sense of hopelessness.

In contrast, spirituality teaches that we are enough just as we are. It encourages self-acceptance and fosters a connection to something greater than ourselves, whether that be a higher power, the universe, or simply a deep sense of purpose. In a world that constantly tells us we need more; spirituality reminds us that we already have what we need within us.

Scientific Evidence of Spirituality's Benefits

This isn't just wishful thinking—there's real science behind the benefits of spirituality. Numerous studies have shown that people with a regular spiritual practice, whether through prayer, meditation, or mindfulness, tend to experience greater emotional well-being and resilience.

In fact, MRI scans of the brain have revealed something fascinating: people with a consistent spiritual practice actually have different brain tissue. A study conducted by Columbia University found that those who engage in regular spiritual practices had thicker brain tissue in the prefrontal cortex, the area of the brain associated with emotional regulation and self-control. This thicker brain tissue helps them manage stress, make better decisions, and navigate challenging emotions more effectively.

Essentially, spirituality rewires our brain for resilience. It helps us cope with life's ups and downs, find meaning in difficult situations, and remain grounded when everything around us feels chaotic.

Now, compare that to social media, which does the opposite. Studies have shown that excessive use of social media is linked to higher levels of anxiety, depression, and loneliness. Instead of thickening our brain tissue and building resilience, social media often exacerbates our insecurities, feeding into a loop of comparison and inadequacy.

The Illusion of Connection

One of the reasons social media has become such a powerful force in our lives is because it offers the illusion of connection. We can DM a friend, like a photo, or comment on a post, and it feels like we're engaging in meaningful interaction. But in reality, these interactions are often shallow and lack the depth needed to foster true connection.

Spirituality, on the other hand, provides a sense of connection that goes beyond surface-level interactions. It connects us to ourselves, to others, and to something greater. Whether it's through prayer, meditation, or simply spending time in nature, spirituality allows us to tap into a deeper level of connection that social media simply can't provide.

Take mindfulness, for example. This practice teaches us to be present in the moment, to fully engage with our thoughts, feelings, and surroundings. When we're mindful, we're able to connect with ourselves on a deeper level and become more attuned to our needs and desires. This kind of introspection is crucial for developing self-awareness and emotional resilience—qualities that are often lacking in a world dominated by social media.

Rediscovering Internal Strength

The question, then, is how do we shift away from seeking validation online and rediscover the internal strength that comes from spirituality?

It starts with awareness. We need to recognize that while social media may provide a quick fix of validation, it's not a sustainable source of self-worth. True self-worth comes from within, and it's something that can be cultivated through spiritual practices like meditation, mindfulness, prayer, or even journaling.

Here are a few ways to start reconnecting with your inner strength:

1. **Limit Social Media Use**: It might seem obvious, but one of the best ways to break free from the validation trap is to simply spend less time on social media. Set boundaries for yourself—whether it's limiting your screen time, taking breaks throughout the day, or even doing a social media detox.

2. **Practice Mindfulness**: Mindfulness is about being present in the moment and fully engaged with your thoughts and emotions. Start by setting aside just a few minutes each day to practice mindfulness, whether it's through meditation, deep breathing, or simply taking a walk in nature.

3. **Cultivate Gratitude**: Spirituality teaches us to focus on what we have rather than what we lack. Practicing gratitude is a powerful way to shift your mindset from one of scarcity to one of abundance. Each day, take a moment to reflect on the things you're grateful for—whether it's your health, your relationships, or even something as simple as a beautiful sunset.

4. **Engage in a Spiritual Practice**: Whether it's prayer, meditation, or attending religious services, engaging in a spiritual practice can help you reconnect with your inner strength and find meaning in your life. Don't worry about doing it "right"—the key is to find what works for you and stick with it.

5. **Find Community**: One of the most powerful aspects of spirituality is the sense of community it provides. Whether it's through a religious group, a meditation circle, or even an online community of like-minded individuals, finding a

group of people who share your values can provide support, encouragement, and a sense of belonging.

Wrapping it Up: Filling the Void

Social media may have its perks, but it's no substitute for the deep sense of purpose and connection that comes from spirituality. As we continue to navigate this digital age, it's crucial that we find ways to balance our online presence with practices that nourish our souls.

By reconnecting with spirituality—whatever that means for you—we can begin to fill the void that social media leaves behind. We can cultivate inner strength, find meaning in our lives, and learn to validate ourselves from within, rather than seeking approval from a screen.

CHAPTER SIX

Anxiety Nation: Have We Normalized It?

Anxiety is everywhere. It's on the news, in our conversations, and even in our memes. It seems like everyone is feeling anxious about something, whether it's climate change, the economy, relationships, or just life in general. But here's the thing: while it's completely normal to feel anxious every now and then, we've reached a point where anxiety has become so normalized that it's almost worn like a badge of honor. You know, that whole "I'm so stressed out, I have so much going on" flex. And while it's important to acknowledge that anxiety is real and affects millions of people, we need to take a step back and ask ourselves—is normalizing anxiety really helping us, or is it making things worse?

The Rise of the Anxious Identity

In today's fast-paced world, where everything feels urgent and overwhelming, anxiety has become a common emotional response. But what's troubling is how it's slowly become a defining characteristic for many people, especially younger generations. Scroll through social media, and you'll see countless posts with captions like, "My anxiety could never" or "Anxiety life," accompanied by a quirky gif or a relatable meme. It's almost as if having anxiety is part of the personality checklist these days, right alongside being a coffee lover and binge-watching Netflix.

While these lighthearted posts can help people feel less alone, they also blur the lines between normal stress and clinical anxiety. By constantly reinforcing the idea that *everyone* is anxious, we risk trivializing the experience for those who are actually dealing with an anxiety disorder. More than that, we risk accepting anxiety as just another part of life—something to live with rather than something to overcome.

Anxiety as a Status Symbol

The hustle culture has played a big part in making anxiety seem like a status symbol. We've all heard the phrase, "If you're not stressed, you're not working hard enough." In this productivity-obsessed culture, being calm and relaxed is almost seen as a sign of laziness or lack of ambition. Everyone's supposed to be "grinding" or "hustling," and if you're not, well, you must not be doing enough.

This pressure to constantly be doing more feeds directly into anxiety. People feel guilty when they're not busy, even though being constantly busy is what leads to burnout in the first place. It's a vicious cycle: the more we glorify being overwhelmed and frazzled, the more anxious we become. And instead of recognizing this for the unhealthy mindset it is, we start to wear our anxiety like a badge of honor—proof that we're "doing life" the right way. But guess what? Life isn't supposed to feel like a never-ending race, and anxiety shouldn't be the cost of entry into adulthood.

How Did We Get Here?

So, how did we get to this point where anxiety is so pervasive and normalized? There are a few key factors at play:

1. **The Pace of Modern Life**: Everything moves faster today than it did even ten years ago. From the speed of information to the expectations at work, we're constantly bombarded with more than we can handle. With smartphones in our pockets, the world never turns off. This constant stimulation doesn't give our brains time to relax, contributing to higher levels of anxiety across the board.

2. **Social Media's Role**: Social media has turned comparison into a full-time activity. Everyone's life looks perfect through the filter of Instagram or TikTok, but when you're constantly comparing your behind-the-scenes to someone else's highlight reel, it's no wonder anxiety is on the rise. We worry about not measuring up, not being good enough, and missing out—further fueling the anxiety fire.

3. **Economic Pressures**: Let's be real—the economy is stressful. Wages haven't kept up with the cost of living, student debt is through the roof, and housing prices are climbing. These pressures make it difficult for people, especially younger generations, to feel secure, adding to an underlying sense of anxiety about the future.

4. **The Stigma Around Mental Health**: While we've made strides in opening up conversations about mental health, there's still a stigma attached to seeking help for anxiety. Many people feel like they should be able to "handle it" on their own, which often leads to them bottling up their emotions until they reach a breaking point.

5. **Trauma from Global Events**: The world isn't short on crises—whether it's the COVID-19 pandemic, climate change, or political instability, global events are triggering anxiety on a mass scale. When the world feels like it's falling apart, it's hard to keep your anxiety in check.

When Anxiety Becomes the Norm

The problem with normalizing anxiety is that it starts to feel like an inevitable part of life. We tell ourselves, "Of course I'm anxious, who isn't?" and then we just live with it, accepting it as our baseline emotional state. But this is dangerous. When we normalize anxiety, we rob ourselves of the opportunity to address it and, more importantly, to build resilience against it.

Resilience is our ability to bounce back from stress and adversity. It's the emotional muscle that allows us to face life's challenges without being overwhelmed. But if we're constantly accepting anxiety as normal, we're not building resilience—we're letting it weaken us. And without resilience, every bump in the road feels like a mountain.

Breaking the Cycle: Moving Beyond Anxiety

So, how do we break free from this cycle of normalized anxiety? How do we stop wearing it like a badge of honor and start seeing it for what it is—a barrier to living a full and fulfilling life? Here are a few ways to start:

1. **Recognize Anxiety for What It Is**: Not all stress is anxiety, and not all anxiety is bad. It's important to differentiate between everyday stress and clinical anxiety. Stress is a normal part of life, and it can even be motivating in small doses. But when stress becomes chronic and starts to interfere with your daily life, that's when it's time to take a closer look.
2. **Stop Glorifying Stress**: It's time to put an end to the idea that being stressed or anxious means you're successful. Success isn't about how much you can juggle or how overwhelmed you feel—it's about balance, fulfillment, and well-being. We need to stop equating stress with achievement and start recognizing the value of calm, peace, and rest.
3. **Unplug from the Comparison Game**: Social media can be a breeding ground for anxiety. If scrolling through Instagram leaves you feeling like you're not good enough or missing out, it's time to take a break. Unplug for a day or two, and remind yourself that social media isn't real life. Focus on your own journey and let go of the need to compare yourself to others.
4. **Seek Professional Help**: There's no shame in seeking help if anxiety is taking over your life. Therapy, counseling, or even talking to a trusted friend can make a world of difference. Cognitive-behavioral therapy (CBT) is especially effective in helping people manage anxiety by

teaching them how to reframe their thoughts and behaviors.

5. **Build Resilience**: Resilience isn't something you're born with—it's something you develop over time. Start small by facing challenges head-on instead of avoiding them. Learn coping strategies, practice mindfulness, and remind yourself that you're stronger than you think. Each time you overcome a challenge, you're building your resilience muscle.
6. **Practice Mindfulness**: Anxiety thrives on future-oriented thinking—worrying about what *might* happen instead of focusing on what's happening right now. Mindfulness is the practice of being present in the moment and can be incredibly helpful in calming anxiety. Even just a few minutes a day of mindfulness meditation can help reduce anxious thoughts and bring a sense of calm.

Wrapping it Up: Reclaiming Peace

At the end of the day, we have to stop accepting anxiety as an inevitable part of life. It's not something to embrace or wear as a status symbol. Instead, we need to view anxiety for what it is—a signal that something needs attention. By addressing it head-on, building resilience, and prioritizing mental health, we can reclaim the peace and calm that anxiety tries to steal from us.

Life is hard, but it doesn't have to be anxiety-inducing. We can choose a different way—a way that involves resilience, mindfulness, and the courage to face challenges without letting them consume us. It's time to stop letting anxiety define us and start living a life that's truly free from its grip.

CHAPTER SEVEN

The Over-Diagnosis of Trauma

Trauma is real. It's painful, it's complex, and it has lasting effects on people's lives. But in recent years, the term *trauma* has been stretched so far beyond its original meaning that it's now being applied to almost any emotional struggle. While there's no doubt that we need to take trauma seriously, the over-diagnosis of trauma, especially in children, can have unintended consequences. Instead of fostering resilience and teaching young people how to cope with the inevitable challenges of life, we risk creating a generation that is overly dependent on labeling every negative experience as trauma, making it harder for them to bounce back from adversity.

Trauma vs. Adversity: Understanding the Difference

To start, we need to clarify the difference between trauma and adversity. Trauma is a deeply distressing or disturbing experience, often with long-term psychological consequences. Adversity, on the other hand, refers to difficulties or misfortune. Adversity is a part of life. Everyone will experience it at some point—whether it's failing a test, losing a loved one, or going through a rough breakup. These moments of adversity, while painful, are opportunities for growth. They build resilience, strengthen our coping mechanisms, and prepare us for the inevitable challenges that life will throw our way.

Trauma, however, is on a different level. It involves significant emotional or physical harm and often requires professional intervention. But here's the issue: we've started to blur the line between trauma and adversity. Every difficult moment is now being treated as traumatic, and this shift in thinking is impacting how we handle emotional struggles.

When Everything is Trauma, Nothing Is

In recent years, the word *trauma* has become a go-to label for almost any negative experience. Didn't get invited to a party? That's traumatic. Lost a game at school? Traumatizing. Struggled with anxiety during a tough exam? You must have been traumatized by the pressure.

While it's important to recognize that emotional pain is real and valid, slapping the trauma label on every hardship is not helpful. In fact, it does the opposite of what we intend. By labeling everyday difficulties as trauma, we dilute the meaning of the word and overlook those who have truly experienced life-altering events.

Even worse, when children are taught to view every setback as a traumatic event, they begin to internalize the idea that they are fragile, broken, and incapable of handling life's challenges. This mindset robs them of the opportunity to develop essential coping skills. Instead of learning how to deal with failure, disappointment, or hardship, they are conditioned to believe that these experiences are too overwhelming to manage.

The Role of Parents and Society

Parents, educators, and mental health professionals play a crucial role in how children understand and respond to adversity. The rise of the "trauma culture" is partly fueled by well-meaning adults who are eager to protect their children from emotional pain. It's understandable—no parent wants to see their child suffer. But by stepping in too quickly, labeling every difficult experience as traumatic, and shielding children from discomfort, we inadvertently send the message that they are not capable of handling life's ups and downs.

The reality is, life is full of challenges. Whether it's navigating a tough social situation at school, dealing with a demanding teacher, or facing rejection, kids need to learn how to cope with these experiences in healthy ways. Labeling these moments as trauma doesn't help them—it holds them back.

The Consequences of Over-Diagnosis

Over-diagnosing trauma has real consequences, both for the individual child and for society as a whole. Here are a few of the unintended outcomes:

1. **Creating a Victim Mentality**: When children are taught to see themselves as victims of trauma in every difficult situation, they develop a victim mentality. Instead of feeling empowered to take control of their emotions and actions, they may feel helpless and dependent on others to "fix" their problems. This mindset limits their potential and can have long-term effects on their confidence and ability to navigate adult life.

2. **Avoiding Responsibility**: The trauma label can sometimes be used as an excuse to avoid responsibility. For example, if a child struggles academically or has behavioral issues, it might be tempting to attribute those difficulties to trauma instead of addressing underlying issues like poor study habits or a lack of discipline. While trauma can certainly impact behavior, it's important to balance that understanding with personal responsibility and accountability.

3. **Undermining Resilience**: Resilience is the ability to bounce back from hardship. It's what allows people to pick themselves up after failure and keep moving forward. But if children are constantly told that their struggles are traumatic, they may begin to believe that they are too fragile to overcome challenges. This undermines their ability to build resilience and develop the emotional strength they need to thrive in life.

4. **Flooding Mental Health Services**: The over-diagnosis of trauma has also contributed to the flooding of mental health services. While therapy is an incredibly valuable resource for those who need it, the overuse of trauma diagnoses has led to long wait times and overburdened systems. This can make it harder for individuals who are dealing with true trauma to access the help they need.

The Importance of Context

To be clear, trauma is real, and many people—children and adults alike—experience it. Whether it's the result of abuse, neglect, violence, or other extreme circumstances, trauma can have lasting effects on mental and emotional well-being. It's important that we continue to acknowledge and treat genuine trauma with the care and attention it deserves.

But we also need to be mindful of the context. Not every difficult experience is traumatic, and not every emotional struggle requires a diagnosis. Sometimes, kids are just going through a rough patch. Sometimes, they need to be encouraged to face their fears, work through their problems, and come out stronger on the other side.

As adults, it's our job to provide children with the tools they need to navigate life's challenges. This means helping them differentiate between trauma and adversity, offering support without shielding them from every hardship, and encouraging them to develop resilience rather than reinforcing a victim mindset.

Building Coping Skills

So, how can we help kids develop coping skills without over-diagnosing trauma? Here are a few strategies:

1. **Teach Emotional Regulation**: Kids need to learn how to manage their emotions in healthy ways. This includes recognizing when they're feeling overwhelmed, understanding why they feel that way, and finding strategies to calm down and refocus. Mindfulness exercises, breathing techniques, and journaling can all be helpful tools.

2. **Encourage Problem-Solving**: When kids face challenges, resist the urge to jump in and solve the problem for them. Instead, guide them through the process of figuring it out on their own. Ask questions like, "What do you think would help in this situation?" or "What's a small step you could take to move forward?"

3. **Normalize Failure**: Failure is a part of life, and it's important that kids understand that it's okay to fail. In fact, failure is often the best teacher. Encourage kids to take risks, try new things, and view failure as an opportunity to learn and grow.

4. **Foster a Growth Mindset**: A growth mindset is the belief that abilities and intelligence can be developed through hard work and perseverance. Help kids adopt this mindset by praising effort rather than outcomes, and by encouraging them to keep trying, even when things get tough.

5. **Model Resilience**: Kids learn by watching the adults in their lives. If they see you handling stress and adversity with resilience, they'll be more likely to do the same. Be open about your own challenges and show them how you work through difficult situations in healthy ways.

Moving Forward: Redefining Trauma and Adversity

As we move forward, we need to be more intentional about how we use the term *trauma*. While it's important to acknowledge the emotional struggles that children face, we also need to give them the tools to handle those struggles without immediately labeling them as traumatic.

By teaching kids to differentiate between trauma and adversity, helping them build resilience, and encouraging them to face life's challenges head-on, we can create a generation that is not only emotionally strong but also capable of thriving in the face of adversity. Trauma is real, but so is resilience—and it's time we started focusing more on the latter.

CHAPTER EIGHT

Rising Above: Redefining Toughness

When you hear the word *tough*, what comes to mind? For many, toughness is often associated with being stoic, emotionless, and able to handle anything life throws at you without so much as a tear. It's about gritting your teeth, putting your head down, and powering through. But here's the thing—real toughness isn't about being robotic or pretending that life's challenges don't affect you. True toughness is about facing adversity with grace, grit, and vulnerability. It's about acknowledging your emotions, embracing challenges, and rising above them.

It's time to redefine what it means to be tough and reclaim resilience in a way that allows us to face the world with strength, compassion, and emotional intelligence.

The Misconception of Toughness

For generations, toughness has been framed as emotional suppression. The cultural message, particularly for boys and men, has been, "Don't cry. Don't show weakness. Be tough." This idea of toughness—where emotions are seen as a liability and vulnerability as weakness—has led to a culture where asking for help, admitting fear, or showing emotion is often stigmatized.

In the process, we've created a very narrow, incomplete picture of what toughness really is. Suppressing emotions doesn't make someone tough; it just makes them disconnected from their own feelings. Ignoring adversity doesn't build resilience; it just creates a façade that hides the real struggles beneath the surface.

The truth is, life is hard. Challenges, loss, failure, and pain are inevitable. Pretending they don't affect you doesn't make you stronger; it just delays the healing process and erodes your emotional well-being. True toughness is about facing those challenges head-on, with the understanding that it's okay to feel and to struggle, but it's essential to rise above.

Redefining Toughness: Emotional Strength Meets Grit

Let's redefine toughness, shall we? Instead of thinking of it as emotional stoicism, let's start thinking about toughness in terms of resilience. Resilience is the ability to bounce back from adversity, to recover from setbacks, and to keep moving forward even when the path ahead is difficult. It's about understanding that life's challenges aren't meant to be avoided—they're meant to be faced with courage and determination.

Being tough isn't about ignoring your feelings; it's about having the emotional strength to acknowledge them, process them, and keep going. In fact, toughness is about allowing yourself to feel all the emotions that come with hardship—sadness, frustration, anger, even fear—and then using those emotions to fuel your perseverance.

Toughness means allowing yourself to be vulnerable, to admit when you're struggling, and to ask for help when you need it. Vulnerability isn't the opposite of toughness—it's a crucial part of it. By acknowledging our own vulnerability, we open ourselves up to growth, connection, and true strength.

Toughness in the Face of Failure

Failure is an inevitable part of life. It's something we all experience at one point or another, and how we respond to failure often determines our future success. For too long, toughness has been equated with the ability to power through failure without flinching. But true toughness comes not from avoiding failure, but from embracing it as a learning experience.

When we redefine toughness, failure is no longer something to be feared—it's something to be valued. Failure teaches us resilience, perseverance, and creativity. It challenges us to rethink our approach and come back stronger. Instead of seeing failure as the end of the road, we can begin to see it as a stepping stone on the path to growth.

Take a look at some of the most successful people in the world—athletes, entrepreneurs, artists, and leaders. Their success stories are often littered with failures, setbacks, and roadblocks. What sets them apart isn't their ability to avoid failure; it's their ability to face it, learn from it, and keep going.

So, the next time you experience failure, don't see it as a personal flaw or a sign that you're not good enough. Instead, view it as an opportunity to build your toughness. Reflect on what went wrong, learn from the experience, and use it to fuel your next attempt. That's real resilience.

Toughness in Vulnerability

One of the most powerful ways to redefine toughness is to embrace vulnerability. We've been conditioned to believe that being tough means keeping our emotions hidden, never letting anyone see our weaknesses. But the reality is that vulnerability is a sign of strength, not weakness.

It takes courage to show up fully as yourself, with all your flaws, fears, and uncertainties. It takes even more courage to share those parts of yourself with others. Whether it's admitting that you're struggling, asking for support, or opening up about a personal failure, vulnerability is one of the bravest things you can do.

In her groundbreaking work on vulnerability, researcher and author Brené Brown has shown that vulnerability is at the heart of meaningful human connection. When we allow ourselves to be vulnerable, we create deeper, more authentic relationships with others. We also give ourselves permission to grow and evolve, rather than pretending that we have it all figured out.

Being tough doesn't mean you have to go it alone. In fact, one of the hallmarks of true toughness is the willingness to lean on others when you need support. Asking for help is not a sign of weakness—it's a sign of self-awareness and emotional intelligence. It takes real strength to admit that you can't do everything on your own, and to seek out the resources and relationships that can help you through tough times.

Grace in the Face of Adversity

Another key element of toughness is grace. When life throws challenges our way, it's easy to react with anger, frustration, or bitterness. But true toughness is about responding to adversity with grace, even when it feels impossible. This doesn't mean suppressing your emotions or pretending that everything is fine. It means finding a way to navigate tough situations with dignity, humility, and perseverance.

Grace is about staying grounded, even when life feels chaotic. It's about recognizing that adversity is a part of life, and that you have the inner strength to weather the storm. When we approach challenges with grace, we're able to stay focused on what matters most and keep moving forward, even when things aren't going our way.

One of the most powerful ways to cultivate grace is through self-compassion. Toughness isn't about being hard on yourself—it's about being kind to yourself, especially in the face of adversity. When you treat yourself with compassion, you're better equipped to handle challenges with resilience and grace. You give yourself the space to heal, to grow, and to rise above.

Grit: The Power of Perseverance

If toughness is about emotional strength and grace, then grit is about perseverance. Grit is what keeps you going when the going gets tough. It's the determination to keep putting one foot in front of the other, even when the road ahead feels long and uncertain.

Grit is the engine that drives resilience. It's what allows you to push through setbacks, disappointments, and failures without losing sight of your goals. Grit isn't about bulldozing through life without feeling—it's about staying committed to your purpose, even when things get difficult.

In her book *Grit: The Power of Passion and Perseverance*, psychologist Angela Duckworth explains that grit is one of the most important predictors of success. It's not talent, intelligence, or luck that determines who will succeed—it's grit. People with grit are able to maintain their focus and motivation over the long haul, even when they encounter obstacles.

Grit is about persistence. It's about understanding that success is rarely achieved overnight, and that the path to your goals is often filled with detours, setbacks, and roadblocks. But with grit, you keep going. You stay focused, stay determined, and keep showing up, even when the journey feels hard.

Rising Above: Toughness and Resilience

As we redefine toughness, it's important to remember that toughness and resilience go hand in hand. Toughness isn't about avoiding adversity—it's about rising above it. It's about facing life's challenges with emotional strength, vulnerability, grace, and grit. It's about embracing failure as a learning experience, showing up fully as yourself, and persevering even when the road gets rocky.

In a world that often equates toughness with emotional suppression, we have the opportunity to redefine what it really means to be strong. True toughness is about resilience. It's about bending without breaking, adapting to challenges, and continuing to move forward, no matter what life throws your way.

So let's rise above the outdated definitions of toughness that tell us to hide our emotions and avoid our struggles. Let's embrace a new kind of toughness—one that is rooted in vulnerability, grace, and perseverance. Because real toughness isn't about pretending that life is easy—it's about rising above life's challenges with strength, courage, and resilience.

CHAPTER NINE

How Did We Survive? Lessons from Gen X

We are the "latchkey" generation. Gen Xers, born between the mid-1960s and early 1980s, grew up in a world without smartphones, helicopter parents, or constant supervision. We were the kids who walked home from school, let ourselves in with a key around our necks, and figured things out on our own. There wasn't someone always hovering to make sure we didn't fall, and when we did fall—literally or figuratively—we learned how to get back up.

Today, people look back at the way we were raised with a mixture of awe and disbelief. *You let an 8-year-old take care of themselves for hours at a time?* Yes, we did. And guess what? We survived. Not only that, but we learned some pretty valuable lessons about resilience, independence, and grit along the way.

The Latchkey Life: A Crash Course in Independence

If you grew up in the '70s, '80s, or even early '90s, you likely experienced the "latchkey" life. It wasn't uncommon for kids to be left alone for hours after school while their parents worked. The term *latchkey kids* became widely used to describe children who let themselves in the house after school, often with minimal adult supervision. And, in hindsight, it was a crash course in independence.

Back then, the idea of kids being alone wasn't considered neglectful; it was just how things were. Many households had both parents working, so children had to learn to navigate the world without someone constantly looking over their shoulders. You were expected to lock the door, make yourself a snack, finish your homework, and entertain yourself—sometimes until dinnertime.

Without constant parental supervision, we learned how to figure things out on our own. Did something break? You tried to fix it before Mom and Dad got home. Did you forget to bring a form to school? You learned to manage the consequences. These moments of self-reliance were small but significant building blocks in our journey toward becoming independent adults. And while some may view it as a "sink or swim" upbringing, the majority of us swam—maybe not gracefully at first, but we made it to shore.

Learning to Solve Problems Without Google

Imagine this: It's 1985. You come home from school, and the microwave won't turn on. There's no smartphone to Google the solution, no app to troubleshoot for you. What do you do? You tinker with it. You unplug it, plug it back in, maybe even get a screwdriver out to see if you can figure it out. If all else fails, you wait until someone who knows better gets home.

This was everyday life for us. We didn't have the luxury of instant answers. If you needed help with your homework, you either figured it out yourself, asked a friend, or—gasp—waited until the next day to ask your teacher. Patience and problem-solving were part of the deal.

Fast forward to today, where every question can be answered in seconds with a quick internet search. While technology has made life undeniably easier, it has also robbed many young people of the opportunity to develop problem-solving skills. When everything is handed to you at the click of a button, you don't get as much practice in figuring things out for yourself. For Gen X, learning to problem-solve without instant answers was just part of growing up, and it made us more resourceful as a result.

The Absence of Helicopter Parents

Helicopter parenting wasn't even a concept when we were kids. Parents loved us, but they weren't micromanaging our every move. If you forgot your lunch, you either went hungry or borrowed some food from a friend. If you got into a fight at school, your parents didn't swoop in to resolve it for you. They let you handle it. This wasn't because they didn't care—it was because they trusted us to figure things out.

The absence of helicopter parenting gave us the freedom to make mistakes and learn from them. We weren't shielded from the consequences of our actions, and as a result, we learned personal responsibility. If you failed a test, it wasn't because the teacher was unfair or because your parents didn't help you enough. It was because you didn't study enough, and that was something you had to own.

That sense of ownership over our successes and failures shaped us into resilient adults. We understood that life wasn't always going to be fair, and when things didn't go our way, we didn't fall apart. Instead, we adapted, regrouped, and kept moving forward. Helicopter parenting, for all its good intentions, removes that learning opportunity from kids today. When someone is always there to catch you, you never learn how to pick yourself up after a fall.

Navigating Social Life Without a Safety Net

Navigating social life as a Gen Xer was, to put it mildly, an adventure. We didn't have social media, so every friendship, argument, and interaction happened in real time. If you wanted to hang out with someone after school, you called them—on a landline. If you got into a fight with a friend, you had to deal with it face-to-face. There were no text messages or DMs to hide behind.

When conflicts arose, we didn't have the option to ghost someone online or craft the perfect response after hours of thought. We had to resolve issues on the spot. This built social resilience. We learned how to negotiate, how to handle rejection, and how to stand up for ourselves without someone stepping in to mediate.

Today's kids, by contrast, often rely on digital communication for much of their social interaction. While it's made it easier to stay connected, it's also made it easier to avoid difficult conversations. When you can edit your responses or hide behind a screen, you miss out on the raw, in-the-moment lessons that come with face-to-face conflict resolution. Gen X didn't have that safety net, and it made us more comfortable navigating social situations—both good and bad.

Taking Risks and Learning from Failure

Growing up, we took risks that might make today's parents gasp in horror. We rode our bikes without helmets, climbed trees without supervision, and spent hours playing outside, often out of sight from adults. These weren't reckless acts; they were rites of passage. We learned to assess risks, to push our limits, and, yes, sometimes to fail spectacularly.

But those failures taught us valuable lessons. When you fell off your bike, you learned to be more careful. When you made an unwise decision at school, you faced the consequences. Failure wasn't something to be avoided at all costs—it was part of the learning process. And through those failures, we built resilience.

Today, many kids are shielded from failure to the point where they never have the chance to experience it. Parents intervene to ensure their children never stumble, but in doing so, they deprive them of the opportunity to learn from their mistakes. Gen X learned early on that failure was inevitable, but it wasn't something to fear. It was something to grow from.

The Self-Reliance Generation

One of the defining characteristics of Gen X is self-reliance. We had to learn how to take care of ourselves from an early age. Whether it was making dinner, doing chores, or navigating the difficulties of school life, we were expected to be responsible for ourselves.

This sense of self-reliance has carried over into adulthood. Many Gen Xers have built careers, families, and lives based on the principles they learned as latchkey kids. We're adaptable, resourceful, and not afraid to roll up our sleeves and get to work when life throws us a curveball.

But self-reliance is more than just being able to take care of yourself—it's about having confidence in your own abilities. Growing up in an environment where we were trusted to figure things out gave us a sense of competence and autonomy. We didn't wait for someone else to solve our problems; we took action.

Lessons for Today

So, what can today's generation learn from Gen X? There are a few key lessons that can be applied to how we raise children today:

1. **Let Kids Figure Things Out**: Kids need to experience small failures and challenges in order to develop resilience. Instead of swooping in to solve every problem, give them the space to figure it out on their own. Whether it's resolving a conflict with a friend or dealing with a forgotten assignment, these moments build problem-solving skills and confidence.
2. **Teach Personal Responsibility**: It's important for kids to understand that their actions have consequences. Encourage personal responsibility by letting them face the natural outcomes of their decisions. If they don't study for a test, they'll learn from the grade they receive. If they forget their lunch, they'll be more likely to remember it next time.
3. **Foster Independence**: Giving kids opportunities to be independent fosters a sense of self-reliance. Whether it's letting them make their own decisions or giving them age-appropriate responsibilities around the house, these experiences teach kids that they are capable of handling life's challenges.
4. **Encourage Risk-Taking (Within Reason)**: Kids need to take risks in order to grow. Encourage them to step out of their comfort zones, whether it's trying a new activity, making new friends, or tackling a difficult project. Risk-taking builds confidence and resilience.

Wrapping it Up: Surviving—and Thriving—as Gen X

Gen X may have grown up in a world without the comforts and conveniences of today, but it was a world that shaped us into resilient, self-reliant adults. We learned how to navigate life's challenges without constant intervention, and those lessons have stayed with us into

CHAPTER TEN

Building Resilience:
A Guide for Parents

Parenting today is not for the faint of heart. In a world that feels more complex, fast-paced, and anxiety-inducing than ever, raising resilient children has become both a necessity and a challenge. Parents now have the critical task of helping their kids develop resilience—the ability to bounce back from setbacks, adapt to tricky situations, and face adversity with strength and grace. Resilience isn't something children are born with; it's a skill that must be nurtured and developed over time.

As parents, it's natural to want to protect our children from hardship. We want to shield them from pain, disappointment, and failure. But the truth is, resilience comes from experiencing and overcoming adversity, not from avoiding it. If we want to raise children who can handle life's inevitable challenges, we need to help them develop the tools to do so. This chapter offers practical steps for building resilience in your children, helping them grow into confident, capable adults who can navigate life's difficulties with grace.

Step 1: Let Them Struggle (A Little)

One of the hardest things for any parent is watching their child struggle. It's natural to want to step in and fix things, to make life easier for them. But if we constantly solve our children's problems, they never learn how to solve problems on their own. Struggling, in manageable doses, is a key part of building resilience.

When your child encounters a challenge—whether it's a difficult homework assignment, a conflict with a friend, or a disappointment in sports—resist the urge to swoop in and fix it. Instead, offer support and guidance, but allow them to work through the problem on their own. This might mean letting them experience frustration, failure, or even tears. And that's okay. These are the moments where resilience is built.

Action Tip: The next time your child faces a problem, ask them questions that encourage problem-solving: "What do you think you should do next?" or "What are some different ways you could approach this?" Let them come up with their own solutions, and then support them as they carry those solutions out.

Step 2: Encourage Risk-Taking (Within Reason)

Children need opportunities to take risks in order to grow. Taking risks—whether it's trying out for the school play, speaking up in class, or making a new friend—helps kids step out of their comfort zones and build confidence. The more they practice taking risks, the more they'll learn to handle the emotions that come with them, like fear, anxiety, and uncertainty.

That being said, risk-taking doesn't mean encouraging reckless behavior. It means allowing your child to try new things and face challenges, knowing that they might fail. When we shield our children from risk, we also shield them from the chance to build resilience.

Action Tip: Create opportunities for your child to take age-appropriate risks. Encourage them to try new activities, speak up for themselves, or take on a responsibility they've never had before. Celebrate their efforts, whether or not they succeed, and talk about what they learned from the experience.

Step 3: Teach Problem-Solving Skills

Resilient children are problem-solvers. They don't crumble in the face of challenges; instead, they look for solutions. As a parent, one of the best things you can do is teach your child how to approach problems with a problem-solving mindset.

When your child encounters a challenge, guide them through the process of figuring out what went wrong, brainstorming workable solutions, and choosing the best course of action. Over time, they'll develop the confidence to tackle problems on their own.

Action Tip: Use everyday challenges as opportunities to practice problem-solving. If your child is struggling with a challenging task, help them break it down into smaller, more manageable steps. Encourage them to think critically about how to approach each step, and remind them that it's okay to make mistakes along the way.

Step 4: Normalize Failure

Failure is a part of life, but many kids today are growing up in environments where failure is avoided at all costs. Whether it's receiving participation trophies for simply showing up or being shielded from the consequences of their actions, kids are often not given the chance to fail. But failure is one of the best teachers in life, and it's an essential part of building resilience.

When children learn that it's okay to fail—and more importantly, that failure is something they can recover from—they become more willing to take risks and try again. They learn that failure isn't something to fear, but something to learn from.

Action Tip: The next time your child fails at something, resist the urge to downplay it or brush it off. Instead, acknowledge their disappointment and then help them reflect on what they can learn from the experience. Ask questions like, "What went wrong?" and "What could you do differently next time?" This approach helps children see failure as a valuable learning opportunity rather than a setback.

Step 5: Foster Emotional Intelligence

Resilience isn't just about handling external challenges—it's also about managing internal emotions. Kids who are emotionally intelligent are better equipped to handle stress, disappointment, and frustration. Emotional intelligence involves recognizing and understanding your own emotions, as well as being able to regulate them effectively.

Teaching emotional intelligence begins with helping children identify their feelings. Instead of telling them to "calm down" or "stop crying," encourage them to name their emotions: "I can see that you're feeling frustrated," or "It sounds like you're really sad about what happened." By acknowledging and validating their feelings, you're helping them build emotional awareness.

Action Tip: Encourage your child to talk about their emotions and model healthy emotional regulation. When you're feeling stressed, for example, explain how you're managing those feelings: "I'm feeling a little overwhelmed right now, so I'm going to take a few deep breaths." This shows your child that it's okay to feel strong emotions, and that there are healthy ways to deal with them.

Step 6: Provide a Strong Support System

Resilience doesn't mean handling everything on your own. In fact, one of the key factors in building resilience is having a strong support system. Children need to know that they have people they can turn to when things get tough—whether that's a parent, teacher, coach, or friend.

While it's important to encourage independence, it's equally important to let your child know that asking for help is a sign of strength, not weakness. When children feel supported, they're more likely to take risks, face challenges, and bounce back from setbacks.

Action Tip: Make it clear to your child that they can come to you for support whenever they need it, but that you're not there to fix everything for them. Let them know that you'll be there to listen, guide, and encourage them, but that they're capable of working through challenges with your support.

Step 7: Model Resilience

As a parent, your actions speak louder than words. If you want to raise resilient children, it's important to model resilience in your own life. When your kids see you facing challenges, handling stress, and bouncing back from setbacks, they learn how to do the same.

When things don't go your way, talk to your children about how you're handling it. Let them see you work through problems, make tough decisions, and keep going, even when life is hard. This not only teaches them resilience but also shows them that challenges are a normal part of life.

Action Tip: The next time you're facing a difficult situation, involve your child in the process of problem-solving. For example, if you're dealing with a setback at work, talk to them about how you're feeling and how you plan to address the issue. This helps them understand that resilience is a skill that even adults need to practice.

Step 8: Celebrate Effort, Not Just Results

In a world that often emphasizes results—grades, trophies, wins—it's important to shift the focus to effort. When children learn to value the process of working hard, rather than just the outcome, they develop a growth mindset. A growth mindset is the belief that abilities can be developed through effort and persistence, and it's a key component of resilience.

When we praise children for their effort, rather than just their achievements, we teach them that success comes from hard work and perseverance. This helps them develop the confidence to keep trying, even when things get difficult.

Action Tip: Instead of praising your child for being smart or talented, focus on praising their effort: "I'm proud of how hard you worked on that project," or "I can see that you didn't give up, even when it was tough." This encourages a growth mindset and reinforces the idea that resilience comes from effort, not innate ability.

Wrapping it Up: Raising Resilient Kids in a Challenging World

Raising resilient children is one of the most important—and rewarding—tasks a parent can undertake. In a world that's constantly changing and full of challenges, resilience is the key to helping kids thrive. By letting your child struggle a little, encouraging risk-taking, teaching problem-solving skills, normalizing failure, fostering emotional intelligence, and modeling resilience yourself, you can help your child develop the strength, confidence, and adaptability they need to handle whatever life throws their way.

Resilience isn't about avoiding hardship—it's about rising above it. And with the right support and guidance, your child can learn to face adversity with grace, grit, and unshakable strength.

CHAPTER ELEVEN

Embracing Adversity: A New Approach to Life

Adversity isn't something to avoid, nor is it something to fear. It's a necessary, inevitable part of life. Whether it comes in the form of a lost job, a failed exam, a difficult relationship, or a life-altering event, adversity is an experience everyone will face at some point. And while adversity is often uncomfortable, even painful, it's through facing and overcoming challenges that we grow, evolve, and build resilience.

What if we shifted our mindset about adversity? What if we stopped seeing it as something that knocks us down and instead viewed it as an opportunity to rise up stronger? By embracing adversity and using it as a tool for growth, both children and adults can develop the resilience, strength, and confidence needed to navigate life's toughest challenges. This chapter will explore practical ways to embrace adversity, reframe failure, and approach life's difficulties with a new perspective.

The Gift of Struggle: Why We Need Adversity

Let's start with a counterintuitive idea: adversity is a gift. It may not feel like it in the moment—after all, who enjoys failing or facing hardship?—but it's often through the most difficult experiences that we discover our true strength and potential. Struggle teaches us lessons that success never could. It shows us our limits, pushes us past them, and reveals what we're truly capable of.

If you think back to some of the most meaningful moments in your life, chances are they weren't the easiest ones. The times you struggled, the moments you doubted yourself, and the challenges you overcame likely shaped you into the person you are today. Adversity builds character. It teaches us resilience, perseverance, and grit.

Yet, so many people spend their lives trying to avoid adversity at all costs. We live in a culture that prizes comfort, ease, and instant gratification, but in doing so, we deprive ourselves of the growth that comes from struggle. When we avoid adversity, we also avoid the chance to grow into the best version of ourselves.

Reframing Failure as a Stepping Stone

One of the biggest obstacles to embracing adversity is our fear of failure. Failure is often seen as a negative experience, something to be avoided or feared. But failure is an essential part of learning and growth. In fact, many of the world's most successful people failed multiple times before they ever succeeded.

Take Thomas Edison, for example. He failed thousands of times before he successfully invented the light bulb. When asked about his failures, Edison famously said, "I have not failed. I've just found 10,000 ways that won't work." His ability to reframe failure as a stepping stone rather than a setback is a perfect example of how embracing adversity can lead to greatness.

When we fail, we're given the opportunity to learn. Failure forces us to evaluate what went wrong, adjust our approach, and try again with new insights. It's through this process of trial and error that we grow, adapt, and ultimately succeed.

Instead of fearing failure, we should learn to embrace it as a necessary part of the journey. Every failure is a lesson in disguise, and each setback brings us one step closer to success.

Action Tip: The next time you or your child experiences failure, take a moment to reflect on what went wrong and what can be learned from the experience. Ask questions like, "What could I have done differently?" and "What will I try next time?" This shifts the focus from the failure itself to the growth that comes from it.

Adversity Builds Resilience

One of the most important benefits of facing adversity is that it builds resilience. Resilience is the ability to bounce back from setbacks and keep moving forward, even when things get tough. It's a critical life skill that allows us to handle challenges with grace and strength.

Resilience doesn't come from avoiding hardship—it's developed through experiencing and overcoming it. Just like a muscle, resilience gets stronger the more it's exercised. Every time we face a challenge, struggle through it, and come out on the other side, we build our resilience muscle. Over time, we become more confident in our ability to handle whatever life throws our way.

For children, building resilience early on sets them up for success later in life. When kids learn that they can handle adversity and come out stronger, they develop a sense of confidence and self-reliance. They're more willing to take risks, try new things, and persevere through difficulties because they know they can bounce back.

Action Tip: Encourage your child to face challenges head-on, rather than avoiding them. Whether it's a difficult school project, a tough conversation with a friend, or trying out for a new sport, remind them that struggle is part of the process and that they are capable of overcoming it.

Adversity Cultivates Empathy

Another often-overlooked benefit of adversity is that it cultivates empathy. When we go through tough times, we develop a deeper understanding of the struggles others face. Adversity teaches us that life isn't always easy, and it helps us connect with others on a more compassionate level.

Children who experience adversity early on are often more empathetic and understanding of others' challenges. They know what it feels like to struggle, and as a result, they're more likely to offer support and encouragement to others going through tough times. Adversity helps them develop emotional intelligence and a sense of compassion for others.

As adults, adversity can help us become better parents, friends, and leaders. When we've faced our own struggles, we're more likely to approach others with kindness and understanding. Adversity reminds us that we're all human, and that everyone is fighting their own battles.

Action Tip: Use adversity as an opportunity to teach empathy. When your child faces a challenge, encourage them to think about how others might feel in similar situations. Ask them questions like, "How do you think your friend feels when they're struggling with this too?" This helps them develop a sense of empathy and compassion for others.

How to Embrace Adversity as a Family

As parents, it's important to model resilience and a positive attitude toward adversity for our children. When they see us handling challenges with grace, they learn how to do the same. Here are some practical ways to embrace adversity as a family:

1. **Talk About Challenges Openly**: Don't shy away from discussing the difficult things that happen in life. Whether it's a setback at work, a health issue, or a family struggle, be open with your children about how you're handling adversity. Let them see that challenges are a normal part of life, and show them how you're working through it.

2. **Celebrate Small Wins**: When you or your child overcomes a challenge, take the time to celebrate the victory, no matter how small. This reinforces the idea that overcoming adversity is something to be proud of and that every step forward is worth celebrating.

3. **Practice Problem-Solving Together**: When a problem arises, whether it's a personal challenge or a family issue, involve your children in the process of finding a solution. Ask for their input, discuss possible solutions, and work together to overcome the challenge. This not only helps them develop problem-solving skills but also shows them that adversity can be tackled as a team.

4. **Reframe Setbacks as Opportunities**: When things don't go as planned, reframe the situation as an opportunity for growth. Instead of focusing on the disappointment, ask your child, "What can we learn from this?" This helps them see adversity as a chance to learn and improve, rather than as a defeat.

5. **Create a Family Resilience Plan**: As a family, discuss how you will handle adversity when it arises. Talk about the importance of staying positive, supporting each other, and focusing on solutions rather than dwelling on problems. Having a resilience plan in place can help your family stay grounded and united during tough times.

Wrapping it Up: A New Approach to Life

Adversity isn't something to be feared or avoided—it's something to be embraced. When we face challenges with an open mind and a willingness to learn, we grow stronger, more resilient, and more compassionate. As parents, helping our children develop the tools to navigate adversity is one of the greatest gifts we can give them. By encouraging them to see challenges as opportunities for growth, we set them up for a life filled with confidence, resilience, and grace.

Adversity is inevitable, but it doesn't have to be something we dread. Instead, let's choose to view it as a powerful teacher—one that helps us discover our inner strength and pushes us to rise above. When we embrace adversity, we embrace life in all its complexity, and we unlock the potential for growth and greatness within ourselves and our children.

CHAPTER TWELVE

From Anxiety to Action: Turning Worry into Wellness

Anxiety. We've all felt it—that buzzing sense of unease that seems to live just below the surface. Some people carry it lightly, like a passing worry, while others wear it like a heavy coat, unable to take it off no matter how warm the day gets. We've touched on how anxiety has not only been normalized but, in some circles, almost glorified. But what happens when that anxiety starts to paralyze us, keeping us stuck in a cycle of worry and inaction? In this chapter, we'll break it down: how anxiety takes root, why it keeps us from moving forward, and, most importantly, how to turn that anxious energy into positive action.

The Paralyzing Effect of Anxiety

Anxiety is like a thief. It sneaks in and robs you of your peace, your energy, and, most destructively, your ability to take action. Whether it's the fear of making a mistake, the worry that you're not good enough, or the overwhelming sense of being out of control, anxiety creates a mental fog that makes even the simplest tasks feel insurmountable.

For many, anxiety manifests as indecision. Do I take that job? Should I apply to that school? What if I fail? These questions swirl in your head, and the fear of making the wrong decision keeps you from making any decision at all. It's like being stuck in quicksand—the more you think about it, the deeper you sink.

Modern life doesn't exactly help. In fact, it seems to encourage anxiety. We're constantly connected, constantly comparing ourselves to others, and constantly bombarded by messages that tell us we should be doing more, achieving more, and living a more perfect version of life. Social media fuels comparison anxiety, the 24-hour news cycle keeps us on edge, and societal pressures push us to be "on" all the time. It's no wonder we feel paralyzed.

And it's not just the big decisions that become overwhelming. Even small, everyday tasks can start to feel impossible when anxiety is in the driver's seat. Think about how anxiety can make something as simple as responding to an email feel like a monumental task. The longer you avoid it, the bigger it becomes in your mind. This is the paralyzing effect of anxiety—it feeds on itself, growing larger and more daunting the longer we let it fester.

The Reality Check: The Cost of Inaction

So, what's the real cost of staying stuck in this cycle of worry and inaction? It's bigger than you think. When anxiety keeps us from taking action, we miss out on opportunities for growth, both personally and professionally. That job we were too scared to apply for? Someone else got it. The friendship we were too anxious to maintain. It fades. The health issue we were too afraid to address? It worsens.

Missed opportunities are one of the most tangible costs of unchecked anxiety. When we avoid taking risks or making decisions, we limit our own potential. Personal growth requires stepping outside of our comfort zones, but anxiety keeps us locked inside them, afraid to venture out.

But the cost isn't just external—it's internal as well. Anxiety, when left unchecked, can strain relationships, both with ourselves and with others. We start to doubt our abilities, lose confidence, and feel increasingly isolated. Relationships with friends, family, or partners can also suffer as anxiety creates distance, either because we're too overwhelmed to communicate or too worried to engage.

And then there's the emotional burnout. Chronic anxiety is exhausting. It wears you down, both mentally and physically. It's not uncommon for people with high levels of anxiety to experience fatigue, headaches, or even more serious health issues. The constant worrying, overthinking, and stress put your body and mind in a state of perpetual tension.

Stories of people trapped in this cycle of anxiety are all too common. Take Amanda, for instance, a 32-year-old graphic designer who spent years too anxious to apply for a promotion at work. She feared rejection, feared failure, feared what others would think if she didn't get the job. So, she did nothing. And while she was busy worrying, her colleague applied for the position and got it. Amanda's anxiety kept her stuck, and the missed opportunity left her feeling defeated, reinforcing the very anxiety that had paralyzed her in the first place.

Embracing Action Over Anxiety

Okay, we've established that anxiety is a problem. But here's the good news: anxiety doesn't have to be permanent. There are ways to move from anxiety to action, to break free from that paralyzing cycle of worry. And they're not as complicated as you might think. Let's dive into some practical, fun, and effective strategies for turning your anxiety into forward momentum.

1. The "5-Minute Rule"

Ever notice how the thought of starting a task is often worse than actually doing it? That's where the "5-Minute Rule" comes in. It's simple: commit to working on something for just five minutes. That's it. Once you've started, you'll often find that it's not as bad as you imagined, and you'll want to keep going. The hardest part of any task is often just getting started, and this little trick helps bypass that mental block.

Let's say you're feeling overwhelmed by your messy kitchen. The thought of cleaning it all is too much, so you keep putting it off. Instead of tackling the entire mess, set a timer for five minutes and start with just one counter. You'll be surprised at how much you can accomplish in those five minutes—and how much easier it feels to keep going once you've started.

2. Mindfulness and Physical Activity

Anxiety thrives on overthinking, and one of the best ways to break the cycle of overthinking is to get out of your head and into your body. Mindfulness practices, such as meditation or deep breathing, can help calm the racing thoughts and bring you back to the present moment. Even just a few minutes of mindful breathing can make a huge difference in how you approach your day.

Physical activity is another great way to reduce anxiety. Whether it's a walk around the block, a yoga session, or a full-on workout, moving your body helps release tension, improve mood, and increase focus. Plus, exercise boosts endorphins, which are your body's natural "feel-good" chemicals.

If you find yourself stuck in a cycle of worry, take a break, and move. Go for a quick jog, stretch, or even do some jumping jacks. It might sound silly, but physical activity can provide the mental reset you need to get unstuck and start taking action.

3. Set Small, Manageable Goals

One of the reasons anxieties feel so overwhelming is that we often set our sights too high. When we focus on the big picture—like landing a dream job or running a marathon—it can feel impossible. But when we break those big goals down into smaller, manageable steps, they become a lot less intimidating.

Let's say your goal is to write a book. Instead of focusing on the daunting task of writing an entire manuscript, start by setting a goal to write just one page a day. It's a small, manageable step that keeps you moving forward without feeling overwhelmed by the enormity of the task.

Breaking down big goals into smaller tasks not only makes them more achievable but also gives you a sense of accomplishment along the way. Each small step you take is progress, and progress builds confidence.

4. Seek Professional Help

There's no shame in asking for help, especially when it comes to managing anxiety. Sometimes, despite our best efforts, anxiety can feel too big to handle on our own. That's where therapy or counseling can make a huge difference. Cognitive-behavioral therapy (CBT), in particular, has been shown to be highly effective in treating anxiety. It helps you identify negative thought patterns and replace them with more positive, action-oriented ones.

Whether it's through therapy, counseling, or even a supportive group, seeking professional help can give you the tools and strategies you need to move from anxiety to action.

Wrapping It Up: Turning Anxiety into Action

Anxiety doesn't have to be the end of the road. It doesn't have to keep you stuck in a cycle of worry and inaction. By using simple strategies like the "5-Minute Rule," practicing mindfulness, setting manageable goals, and seeking help when needed, you can turn anxiety into action and start living a life that's more focused on doing and less on worrying.

Remember, anxiety thrives in the space between thinking and doing. The longer you stay in that space, the bigger the anxiety grows. But when you take action—no matter how small—you break that cycle, regain control, and move forward with confidence.

So, let's take a deep breath, set a small goal, and get started. Five minutes from now, you'll be amazed at how far you've already come.

CHAPTER THIRTEEN

The Power of Failure: Embracing Mistakes as Learning Opportunities

Failure. Just the word itself can stir up discomfort, anxiety, and even dread. We've been conditioned to see failure as something to avoid at all costs, a mark of inadequacy, a reason to give up. But what if we've been looking at failure all wrong? What if failure wasn't something to run from but something to embrace? What if each misstep, each wrong turn, wasn't a dead end but a necessary part of the journey to success? In this chapter, we'll explore the transformative power of failure, why it's essential for growth, and how we can learn to see our mistakes as opportunities rather than obstacles.

Fear of Failure

From a young age, we're taught to fear failure. It starts in school, where mistakes are often met with red marks and low grades, and continues into adulthood, where society glorifies success while sweeping failures under the rug. We're bombarded with images of perfection—Instagram feeds filled with flawless accomplishments, news stories celebrating overnight successes, and social media posts of failing. It feels like a personal indictment, a public declaration of our shortcomings.

The fear of failure is more than just a passing feeling; it can become a crippling mindset. It holds people back from taking risks, pursuing their passions, and stepping outside their comfort zones. Afraid of what might happen if they don't succeed, many people choose to play it safe, opting for the path of least resistance rather than the path that might lead to something greater.

The societal pressure to always succeed is overwhelming. We're expected to have the perfect job, the perfect relationship, the perfect life, and anything less feels like failure. But this relentless pursuit of perfection can stifle creativity, limit personal growth, and lead to stagnation. Fear of failure doesn't just stop us from making mistakes—it stops us from trying altogether.

Yet, without failure, there is no growth. If you never take a risk, you'll never know what you're capable of. If you never make a mistake, you'll never learn the valuable lessons that come from those mistakes. And if you never fail, you'll never experience the immense satisfaction of overcoming failure and achieving something truly remarkable.

The Reality Check: Learning from Mistakes

It's easy to look at successful people and assume that they got there by never failing. But the truth is, behind every great success story is a long list of failures. What sets these individuals apart isn't that they avoided failure—it's that they learned from it, grew from it, and used it as fuel to drive them forward.

Take Thomas Edison, for example. The man famously failed over a thousand times before finally inventing the lightbulb. When asked about his repeated failures, Edison responded, "I have not failed. I've just found 10,000 ways that won't work." His ability to reframe failure as a stepping stone rather than a setback is a powerful lesson in resilience and persistence. Edison didn't see his mistakes as the end of the road; he saw them as part of the process.

Another inspiring example is Oprah Winfrey. Before becoming a media mogul, Oprah faced numerous failures. Early in her career, she was fired from her job as a television news anchor because she was deemed "unfit for TV." That failure could have easily derailed her career, but instead, Oprah used it as a catalyst for growth. She learned from the experience, honed her craft, and eventually built one of the most successful media empires in history. Oprah's story reminds us that failure doesn't define us—it's what we do after we fail that matters.

Research backs this up, too. Studies show that failure is a critical component of success. A study from Northwestern University found that individuals who experienced early-career failures were more likely to succeed in the long run than those who experienced early success. The key difference? Those who failed early learned how to persevere and adapt, skills that proved invaluable as they continued to pursue their goals.

Failures teach us resilience. They show us what doesn't work, help us refine our approach, and force us to become more creative problem-solvers. Every failure is an opportunity to learn, grow, and improve. But in order to benefit from failure, we have to be willing to face it head-on and learn from it, rather than run from it.

Reframing Failure

If failure is such an important part of growth, why do we fear it so much? The answer lies in how we view failure. For most of us, failure feels like an indictment of our abilities or our worth. But what if we shifted that perspective? What if, instead of seeing failure as a final judgment, we saw it as an inevitable part of the journey? What if failure wasn't something to be avoided, but something to be embraced? Here are a few ways to start reframing failure in a way that empowers, rather than discourages, us.

1. Keep a "Failure Journal"

One of the most effective ways to reframe failure is to track it. That's right—celebrate your mistakes by keeping a "Failure Journal." This might sound counterintuitive, but writing down your failures allows you to reflect on them, learn from them, and see how they contributed to your growth. Every time you fail at something—whether it's a work project that didn't go as planned or a personal goal you didn't meet—write it down. Then, write down what you learned from that failure and how you plan to use that lesson moving forward.

Over time, you'll start to see patterns emerge. You'll notice that your failures aren't dead ends; they're just detours that lead to better opportunities. And by documenting your progress, you'll be able to look back and see how far you've come—not despite your failures, but because of them.

2. Turn Setbacks into Stepping Stones

Next time you face a failure or setback, instead of wallowing in it, ask yourself: "What can I learn from this?" Failure isn't something to be ashamed of—it's a chance to gain valuable insights that you wouldn't have otherwise. Maybe you failed a test because you didn't study hard enough. Now you know how to prepare better next time. Maybe a business venture didn't take off. Now you have the experience to tweak your approach and try again with a new strategy.

Failure doesn't have to be the end of the story. In fact, it can be the beginning of something even greater. By seeing each failure as a stepping stone rather than a stumbling block, you can use your mistakes to propel you forward rather than hold you back.

3. Embrace a Growth Mindset

At the heart of reframing failure is adopting a growth mindset. A growth mindset, a term coined by psychologist Carol Dweck, is the belief that abilities and intelligence can be developed through hard work, learning, and perseverance. People with a growth mindset see failure as an opportunity to improve, while those with a fixed mindset see failure as a reflection of their limitations.

By embracing a growth mindset, you'll start to see failure as an essential part of the learning process. Instead of thinking, "I'm not good at this," you'll start thinking, "I'm not good at this *yet*." That small shift in perspective can make a huge difference in how you approach challenges and setbacks.

One way to cultivate a growth mindset is to replace negative self-talk with more positive, constructive language. For example, instead of saying, "I failed, I'll never be good at this," try saying, "I didn't succeed this time, but I can learn and improve." This simple change in wording helps shift your focus from the failure itself to the opportunity for growth.

4. **Learn from the Best**

Some of the most successful people in the world have failed spectacularly—multiple times. They didn't let those failures stop them; they used them as fuel to keep going. Look for examples of people you admire who have faced failure and overcome it. Whether it's a well-known entrepreneur, artist, or athlete, hearing their stories of perseverance can be incredibly motivating.

For example, J.K. Rowling, the author of the *Harry Potter* series, was rejected by twelve different publishers before her first book was finally accepted. If she had given up after the first rejection—or the second, or the tenth—she never would have created one of the most beloved book series of all time. Failure wasn't the end for her; it was just part of the process.

Wrapping It Up: The Power of Embracing Failure

Failure isn't something to fear—it's something to embrace. Every mistake, every setback, and every wrong turn is an opportunity to learn, grow, and improve. When we shift our mindset from avoiding failure to embracing it, we unlock a powerful source of growth and resilience. The road to success is paved with failures, and the people who achieve the most in life aren't the ones who never failed—they're the ones who learned how to fail well.

So the next time you fail (and you will), don't see it as the end of the road. See it as a detour, a lesson, a stepping stone on the path to something greater. Because failure isn't just part of the journey—it's one of the most important parts.

CHAPTER FOURTEEN

Building Strong Relationships: The Importance of Connection and Support

No one gets through life alone. Whether it's through family, friends, colleagues, or partners, our relationships serve as the foundation for resilience and well-being. Strong, supportive relationships are the glue that holds us together during life's most challenging times. They lift us up when we're down, give us strength when we're weak, and provide a sense of belonging that no amount of self-reliance can replace.

In today's world, it might seem like we're more connected than ever. With a swipe, a tap, or a click, we can message a friend, like a photo, or send a heart emoji. But despite these digital connections, many people feel lonelier than ever before. How did we get here? And, more importantly, how can we rebuild the deep, meaningful relationships that help us thrive? This chapter explores the importance of human connection, how modern life has impacted relationships, and how to strengthen personal connections in an increasingly disconnected world.

Isolation and Disconnection

We live in the age of constant connectivity. With smartphones, social media, and messaging apps, we're able to communicate with others more easily than ever before. Yet, despite the ease of staying in touch, many people feel profoundly isolated and disconnected. The paradox of modern life is that the more connected we become online, the more disconnected we often feel in real life.

One of the biggest culprits of this disconnection is technology itself. Social media, in particular, gives us the illusion of connection. We scroll through our feeds, see what our friends are up to, and maybe even comment on their latest post. But these interactions are often shallow and don't provide the same level of emotional connection as face-to-face communication. The endless scrolling can also fuel feelings of loneliness and inadequacy, as we compare our lives to the curated, filtered versions of other people's lives.

In addition to technology, our fast-paced, busy lifestyles contribute to isolation. Many people are working longer hours, commuting further distances, and juggling more responsibilities than ever before. In the hustle of everyday life, relationships often get pushed to the back burner. The result? A growing sense of loneliness and social isolation.

A 2020 study by Cigna found that over 60% of Americans reported feeling lonely, and this number was even higher among younger adults. This "loneliness epidemic" is not just an emotional issue—it's a public health crisis. Research has shown that loneliness and social isolation can have serious consequences for both mental and physical health.

The Reality Check: The Need for Human Connection

It's no secret that relationships are good for us, but the impact of human connection on our health and well-being goes far beyond what most people realize. Strong, supportive relationships are not just a "nice-to-have"—they're essential for our survival.

Research shows that people who have strong social connections are happier, healthier, and live longer than those who are more isolated. In fact, studies have found that the health risks associated with social isolation are comparable to smoking, obesity, and physical inactivity. Social isolation has been linked to increased risks of heart disease, depression, anxiety, and even premature death.

One of the most famous studies on this topic is the Harvard Study of Adult Development, which began tracking the lives of 724 men in 1938. Over 80 years later, the study has shown that the quality of a person's relationships—not wealth, fame, or success—is the single most important predictor of their happiness and longevity. The men who had close, supportive relationships lived longer, healthier lives, while those who were more socially isolated faced greater mental and physical health challenges.

So why are strong relationships so important for our well-being? For one, relationships provide emotional support. When we're going through tough times, having someone to talk to can help us process our feelings, gain perspective, and feel less alone. Strong relationships also provide practical support—whether it's a friend helping you move or a family member offering advice, these connections make life's burdens a little lighter.

But it's not just about support in tough times. Positive social interactions release oxytocin, the "bonding hormone," which reduces stress, lowers blood pressure, and strengthens the immune system. Simply put, human connection makes us feel good, and that feeling has a profound impact on our health and happiness.

Cultivating Meaningful Relationships

In an age where disconnection is more common than connection, how do we go about building and maintaining strong, meaningful relationships? The good news is, it doesn't require grand gestures or complicated strategies. Sometimes, the simplest actions can have the biggest impact. Here are some fun, creative, and practical ways to strengthen your relationships and foster deeper connections in an increasingly disconnected world.

1. The Art of the Regular Check-In

One of the easiest and most effective ways to maintain strong relationships is by checking in regularly with the people you care about. A simple text, phone call, or quick coffee date can go a long way in showing someone that you're thinking of them. You don't have to wait for a special occasion to reach out—just checking in to ask, "How are you really doing?" can open the door to deeper conversations and strengthen your bond.

Pro tip: Set a reminder on your phone or calendar to check in with specific people once a week or once a month. Life gets busy, but taking the time to maintain your relationships is one of the best investments you can make.

2. **Themed Gatherings: Bringing People Together**

Want to spice up your social life? Try hosting themed gatherings. Whether it's a potluck dinner where everyone brings a dish from a different country or a game night with a "retro" theme, hosting fun, themed events can create an inviting atmosphere for connection. Themed gatherings give people something to look forward to and can help break the ice, especially if your group includes a mix of old friends and new acquaintances.

Plus, the shared experience of a fun, lighthearted event can create lasting memories and bring people closer together. And the best part? You don't need to wait for a holiday or birthday to throw a themed gathering—any day can be an excuse to bring people together.

3. **Shared Activities: Strengthening Bonds Through Experiences**

One of the best ways to build deeper connections with others is through shared activities. Whether it's going for a hike, attending a concert, or taking a cooking class together, doing something fun and engaging can strengthen your bond and create opportunities for meaningful conversations.

Physical activities like hiking, walking, or playing sports are particularly effective at fostering connection. Exercise releases endorphins, which improve mood, and participating in a physical activity together can create a sense of teamwork and camaraderie. Even something as simple as going for a walk with a friend can provide the perfect setting for catching up and deepening your relationship.

4. Overcoming Social Anxiety: Taking Small Steps

For those who struggle with social anxiety, building and maintaining relationships can feel daunting. But small steps can make a big difference. Start by reaching out to one person at a time, rather than trying to navigate large social events. Whether it's sending a text to a friend you haven't spoken to in a while or inviting a colleague to grab coffee, taking small, manageable steps can help ease the anxiety of social interaction.

And remember, relationships don't have to be perfect to be meaningful. It's okay to feel nervous or awkward—what matters is showing up and making an effort to connect.

5. The Power of Vulnerability: Building Deeper Connections

If you want to build stronger, more meaningful relationships, one of the most powerful things you can do is be vulnerable. Being open and honest about your thoughts, feelings, and struggles can deepen your connection with others and create a safe space for them to do the same. Vulnerability fosters trust, empathy, and intimacy, all of which are essential ingredients for a strong relationship.

Of course, vulnerability doesn't mean oversharing with everyone you meet. It's about being authentic and allowing yourself to be seen by the people you care about. When you share your true self—flaws, fears, and all—you give others permission to do the same.

Wrapping It Up: Building Strong Relationships in an Age of Disconnection

In a world that often feels disconnected, building strong, meaningful relationships is more important than ever. Relationships are the foundation of resilience—they give us the support, love, and strength we need to navigate life's challenges. And while modern life may make it harder to cultivate those connections, it's far from impossible.

By making small, intentional efforts—whether it's checking in regularly, hosting themed gatherings, or sharing activities with loved ones—you can build and maintain the strong, supportive relationships that are key to your well-being. Remember, it's not about having a huge social circle—it's about nurturing the connections that truly matter.

So, reach out, invite someone over, or simply send that text you've been meaning to send. The people in your life are waiting, and the time to connect is now.

CHAPTER FIFTEEN

Redefining Success: Moving Beyond Societal Expectations

What does success really look like? If we asked society, we'd likely hear the same things over and over: wealth, power, fame, status. The corner office, the six-figure salary, the luxury car, the Instagram-perfect life. But for many, chasing this conventional definition of success leaves them feeling empty, exhausted, and unfulfilled. It's like climbing a ladder only to realize, once you've reached the top, that the ladder was leaning against the wrong wall.

This chapter is about stepping off that ladder and redefining what success means on your own terms. It's about moving beyond the societal pressures that tell us success has to look a certain way and instead crafting a life that aligns with our deepest values, desires, and priorities. True success isn't about what you achieve in the eyes of others—it's about what brings you meaning, fulfillment, and joy.

The Pursuit of Conventional Success

From a young age, we're taught that success is something external—something that can be measured, quantified, and compared. Whether it's the grades we earn in school, the job titles we hold, or the money we make, we're conditioned to believe that success is about achieving more and more. The message is clear: success equals achievement, and achievement equals happiness.

But here's the catch: for many people, chasing conventional success doesn't lead to happiness—it leads to burnout, stress, and dissatisfaction. The pressure to keep climbing higher and higher, to achieve more, earn more, and be more, can feel suffocating. And even when we achieve the things society tells us we should want, it often feels hollow. Sure, the salary is great, but are you actually excited about the work you're doing? The promotion might look impressive on LinkedIn, but does it bring you any closer to the life you truly want?

The pursuit of external success often comes at a cost. In the race to accumulate accolades, we can lose sight of what truly matters—our relationships, our passions, our health, and our sense of self. We push ourselves to the brink, working longer hours, sacrificing personal time, and constantly striving for that next big milestone. But when we get there, the feeling of fulfillment is fleeting, and soon we're back to chasing the next goal, hoping that *this* time, it'll make us feel complete.

This endless pursuit can leave people feeling empty, no matter how much they achieve. Why? Because conventional success is often based on external validation rather than internal fulfillment. When we define success by societal standards—whether it's wealth, power, or prestige—we place our worth in the hands of others. And when our happiness depends on external approval, it's never truly within our control.

The Reality Check: Finding Personal Fulfillment

It doesn't have to be this way. Success doesn't need to be defined by society's standards—it can be defined by *your* standards. True success comes from living a life that's aligned with your values, passions, and priorities. It's about finding fulfillment not in what you achieve, but in how you live.

Take the story of Sam, for example. Sam spent over a decade climbing the corporate ladder in a fast-paced tech company. On paper, she had it all: a high-paying job, a leadership role, and the admiration of her peers. But inside, Sam felt unfulfilled. The long hours and constant pressure left her burnt out and disconnected from the things that brought her joy. She realized that despite her external success, she wasn't truly living the life she wanted.

After much reflection, Sam made the bold decision to step off the corporate treadmill. She downsized her lifestyle, moved to a quieter town, and started a small business doing what she loved—teaching yoga and mindfulness. For Sam, success wasn't about climbing the corporate ladder anymore. It was about living a balanced, peaceful life where she could make a difference in her community and spend time with the people she loved. By redefining success on her own terms, Sam found a deeper sense of fulfillment than she ever had in her high-powered job.

And then there's James, a software engineer who spent years working toward promotions and higher salaries, all the while feeling like something was missing. After a near-burnout, James decided to take a year off to travel and volunteer. He spent time in different communities around the world, teaching kids how to code. What he discovered was that success, for him, wasn't about the paycheck or the accolades—it was about helping others and making a tangible impact. James eventually returned to the tech world but with a new perspective: he prioritized meaningful work and personal well-being over career titles.

These stories aren't about quitting your job or moving to a remote island (though if that's what you want, go for it!). They're about recognizing that success doesn't have to look the way society tells you it should. It's about finding what brings you joy, meaning, and fulfillment—and pursuing that, no matter what the external markers of success may be.

Creating Your Own Definition of Success

So, how do you go about redefining success for yourself? It starts with tuning out the noise of societal expectations and tuning into what matters most to you. Here are some fun and practical exercises to help you create your own personalized definition of success:

1. **The Values Audit**

What are your core values? What matters to you on a deep, personal level? Is it creativity, family, adventure, contribution, freedom? Take some time to reflect on your top values and how they align (or don't align) with your current definition of success. Ask yourself:

- When do I feel most fulfilled?
- What brings me joy and satisfaction, even when there's no external reward?
- What aspects of my life feel most meaningful to me?

Once you've identified your core values, use them as a guide to define success. For example, if family is one of your top values, maybe success means spending quality time with loved ones, rather than working 80-hour weeks. If creativity is important to you, success might involve having time to pursue your artistic passions.

2. The "What If?" Game

This is a great exercise for breaking out of conventional thinking. Ask yourself: "What if money, status, or other people's opinions didn't matter? What would I do with my life?" This question can open up new possibilities and help you discover what you *really* want, not just what you think you should want.

For instance, if you've always dreamed of starting a nonprofit or pursuing a passion project but have been held back by societal expectations, the "What If?" game can help you explore those dreams without judgment. By removing external pressures, you can tap into your true desires and begin to shape a definition of success that's uniquely yours.

3. The Success Spectrum

Society tends to view success as black and white—you're either successful or you're not. But success is a spectrum, and it looks different for everyone. Create your own "Success Spectrum" by listing out the various aspects of your life—career, relationships, health, personal growth, etc.—and define what success looks like in each area.

Maybe in your career, success means finding work that's aligned with your passions, even if it doesn't come with a big paycheck. In relationships, success might mean deepening your connection with friends and family. In personal growth, success could mean learning a new skill or exploring a new hobby.

By defining success across different areas of your life, you create a more balanced, holistic approach to fulfillment. It's not about achieving everything in one area—it's about finding harmony across all aspects of your life.

4. Celebrate Unconventional Wins

Who says success has to be about promotions and pay raises? Start celebrating your "unconventional" wins—the small moments that bring you joy and satisfaction. Maybe it's finishing that book you've been meaning to read, spending an afternoon hiking, or finally getting around to that DIY project at home. Success isn't just about the big milestones; it's about the everyday achievements that make your life richer and more meaningful.

Create a "Win Journal" where you jot down these moments of success—big or small—each day. Over time, you'll start to see that success is less about external validation and more about how you choose to live your life.

Wrapping It Up: Success, Redefined

Redefining success isn't about rejecting ambition or giving up on your goals. It's about aligning your definition of success with what truly matters to you, rather than what society tells you should matter. When you stop chasing other people's version of success and start pursuing your own, you open yourself up to a life that's richer, more fulfilling, and deeply meaningful.

So, what does success look like to *you*? Whether it's having more time for family, pursuing creative passions, making an impact in your community, or simply finding joy in the small moments, the definition is yours to create. And once you redefine success on your own terms, you'll find that it's not about reaching a destination—it's about enjoying the journey every step of the way.

CHAPTER SIXTEEN

Embracing Change: Adapting to Life's Ups and Downs

There's one thing you can always count on in life—change. It's the one constant, the thing that will always show up whether you're ready for it or not. Yet, despite its inevitability, change is something many of us struggle with. It disrupts our routines, forces us out of our comfort zones, and demands that we adapt, whether we like it or not. So why is it so hard to embrace change when we know it's a natural part of life? This chapter is about leaning into the uncertainty, developing flexibility, and learning to see change not as a threat, but as an opportunity for growth.

Resistance to Change

Let's face it: most people don't like change. We like predictability, comfort, and the security of knowing what's coming next. When things change—whether it's a new job, a move to a different city, or an unexpected life event—it can feel unsettling. Our natural response to change is often resistance. We dig in our heels, try to maintain the status quo, and resist the very thing that's pushing us toward growth.

Why is change so hard for so many of us? The answer lies in fear—specifically, fear of the unknown. When we don't know what's coming next, we feel out of control. Our brains are wired to seek safety and familiarity, so when change disrupts that, it triggers stress and anxiety. We start asking, "What if it doesn't work out?" or "What if I fail?" and these worries keep us clinging to the way things are, even when change could bring something better.

Common fears associated with change include:

- **Fear of failure**: What if the new situation doesn't work out, and I end up worse off than before?
- **Fear of loss**: What if I lose what I have now—whether it's a job, relationship, or sense of identity—if things change?
- **Fear of uncertainty**: What if I can't handle the unknown, and I end up overwhelmed or unhappy?

These fears can keep us stuck in situations that no longer serve us. We avoid taking risks, miss out on new opportunities, and, worst of all, limit our own potential for growth. The irony is that change, while scary, is often exactly what we need to move forward.

The Reality Check: The Benefits of Flexibility

Here's the good news: the more flexible we are in the face of change, the more likely we are to thrive. Research shows that people who embrace change and are adaptable tend to be more successful, satisfied, and resilient in life. Flexibility allows us to move through life's ups and downs with grace, rather than being thrown off course by every shift in direction.

Adaptable people tend to see change not as something to fear, but as something to learn from. When we develop a flexible mindset, we're better able to see change as an opportunity rather than a threat. Instead of asking, "What if this goes wrong?" we start asking, "What can I learn from this?" or "How can I grow through this experience?" Flexibility opens the door to new possibilities, allowing us to turn life's unexpected twists into opportunities for personal and professional growth.

Studies in psychology have also shown that flexible people experience lower levels of stress and anxiety. They're more likely to find creative solutions to problems, handle setbacks with resilience, and bounce back from adversity faster. In other words, flexibility isn't just about surviving change—it's about thriving through it.

Navigating Change with Confidence

Now that we know the benefits of embracing change, how do we actually do it? Here are some practical, fun, and witty strategies to help you navigate change with confidence and turn life's curveballs into steppingstones.

1. Goal-Setting: Focus on What You Can Control

Change can feel overwhelming because it often highlights what's outside of our control. But one way to regain a sense of stability is by setting small, achievable goals that give you a sense of direction. Focus on what you *can* control, even if it's something as simple as planning your next steps or identifying what you need to learn for the transition.

For example, if you've just started a new job and feel out of your depth, set a goal to learn one new skill each week or connect with a different colleague every day. These small, manageable goals can help you feel more in control of the changes happening around you and build your confidence in navigating new situations.

2. Seek Support: Don't Go Through It Alone

Change can be isolating, but it doesn't have to be. One of the best ways to handle change is to lean on your support system—whether that's friends, family, mentors, or colleagues. Talking through your fears, getting advice, or simply having someone to listen can make a world of difference.

Remember, seeking support isn't a sign of weakness—it's a sign of strength. By acknowledging that you don't have to go through it alone, you empower yourself to handle change with more confidence. Plus, getting an outside perspective can often reveal opportunities or solutions you hadn't considered.

3. Stay Curious: See Change as an Experiment

Instead of approaching change with dread, what if you approached it with curiosity? What if, instead of worrying about what might go wrong, you asked, "What can I learn from this?" or "What new experience is waiting for me?" Curiosity turns change into an experiment—something to explore, rather than something to avoid.

The next time life throws you a curveball, adopt a mindset of curiosity. Try seeing the unknown as an adventure, a chance to grow and experience something new. Ask yourself: "How can I use this change to expand my skills, my mindset, or my understanding of the world?"

4. Create a "Change Kit": Tools for Tough Transitions

Sometimes, navigating change requires having the right tools in your toolkit. Why not create a "Change Kit" for yourself—a set of resources, practices, and reminders to help you stay grounded when things get turbulent?

Your Change Kit could include:

- **Mindfulness exercises**: Practice deep breathing or meditation to calm your mind during periods of uncertainty.
- **Affirmations**: Positive statements like "I can handle whatever comes my way" can help shift your mindset from fear to confidence.
- **Journaling**: Writing down your thoughts and feelings about the change can help you process them and find clarity.
- **Visual reminders**: Keep a visual cue—like a photo or a quote—that reminds you of your strength and resilience.

By building your own Change Kit, you're equipping yourself with the tools to handle whatever life throws your way.

5. Reframe Setbacks: Change is an Opportunity in Disguise

Not all changes will feel good right away—some might even feel like setbacks. But setbacks can be reframed as opportunities in disguise. Think about the times in your life when a difficult change ended up leading to something better than you imagined.

Maybe that job you didn't get led to a new career path that was more fulfilling. Or that relationship that ended made room for more meaningful connections. Life's ups and downs often lead us to unexpected but valuable outcomes. When you reframe setbacks as opportunities for growth, you're better able to stay positive and motivated during tough transitions.

Wrapping It Up: Embracing Change as a Path to Growth

Change is inevitable, but it doesn't have to be overwhelming. By shifting your mindset from one of resistance to one of flexibility, you can navigate life's ups and downs with confidence and resilience. Instead of seeing change as something to fear, start viewing it as an opportunity for growth—an experiment in learning, adapting, and evolving.

Remember, the key to embracing change is flexibility. When you're able to go with the flow, set small goals, seek support, and stay curious, you open yourself up to a world of new possibilities. Life is constantly in motion, and the more you embrace the ride, the more likely you are to find fulfillment, growth, and success along the way.

CHAPTER SEVENTEEN

Celebrating Small Wins: The Power of Everyday Achievements

In a world that's always pushing us to chase bigger goals, we often forget to take a moment and appreciate the small victories. We set our sights on grand achievements—landing that dream job, reaching a major financial milestone, or launching the next big project—while overlooking the seemingly insignificant steps we take each day. But here's the truth: small wins matter. In fact, they matter more than we often realize. They fuel our motivation, boost our well-being, and keep us moving forward when the big goals seem far out of reach.

This chapter is all about celebrating those small wins—the everyday achievements that we too often dismiss. Because in the journey to success, it's not just the destination that counts. It's every step along the way.

Overlooking Everyday Successes

We live in a culture that glorifies big wins. We celebrate promotions, major life milestones, and headline-worthy accomplishments. But in doing so, we neglect the importance of the small wins that happen every single day—the little moments of progress that often go unnoticed but are essential to our overall success.

When we're constantly focused on the next big thing, we're setting ourselves up for burnout. The pressure to achieve major goals, especially if they're long-term, can feel overwhelming. And when we don't take the time to celebrate the smaller steps that get us there, we miss out on opportunities to feel good about the progress we're making.

This mindset of "bigger is better" can lead to decreased motivation. When we only measure success by big outcomes, the journey starts to feel like an endless grind. We feel like we're not accomplishing anything, even though we're making progress every day. This leads to frustration, exhaustion, and, ultimately, burnout.

Let's take a simple example: imagine you're trying to write a book. If you're only focused on the final product—finishing that 300-page manuscript—it can feel impossible to get started. But if you celebrate every page you write, every chapter you complete, suddenly, the task feels more manageable. You see progress, and that progress fuels your motivation to keep going.

The same principle applies to all aspects of life—whether you're working on a big project at work, trying to get fit, or learning a new skill. Celebrating the small wins along the way is crucial for staying motivated and avoiding burnout.

The Reality Check: The Importance of Recognition

Recognizing small wins isn't just a feel-good strategy—it's backed by science. Psychologists have long known that small wins can have a powerful impact on our mental and emotional well-being. When we acknowledge even the tiniest accomplishments, we activate the brain's reward center, releasing dopamine, the "feel-good" chemical that boosts motivation and helps reinforce positive behavior.

Research shows that people who regularly recognize and celebrate small achievements are more likely to stay committed to their goals. This is because celebrating progress creates a sense of momentum—it reminds us that we're moving forward, even if the finish line is still far away.

A study published in the *Harvard Business Review* found that one of the most important factors in staying motivated at work is making consistent progress in meaningful tasks. The researchers called it the "progress principle." They found that when people tracked their small wins—whether it was solving a minor problem, finishing a small task, or learning something new—they felt more motivated and satisfied with their work.

This idea isn't limited to professional settings. In everyday life, recognizing small wins can help us stay motivated to reach personal goals, improve our relationships, and take better care of our mental health. It shifts our focus from what we *haven't* accomplished yet to what we *have* accomplished, providing a much-needed boost in confidence and energy.

Making Small Wins Matter

Now that we know why celebrating small wins is important, let's talk about how to do it. Here are some creative, fun, and simple ways to start recognizing and celebrating those everyday victories that deserve a little applause.

1. Create a "Win Journal"

A "Win Journal" is an easy and effective way to track and celebrate your small wins. Every day, write down one or two things you accomplished, no matter how small. It could be as simple as sending that email you've been putting off, finishing a workout, or spending 10 minutes reading a book.

Not only does this practice help you reflect on your progress, but it also creates a tangible record of your achievements. On tough days, when it feels like you're not getting anywhere, you can look back at your Win Journal and see just how far you've come.

Pro tip: To make it even more fun, personalize your Win Journal with colorful markers, stickers, or doodles. It's your personal celebration space—make it something you look forward to updating!

2. Host Mini-Celebrations

Why wait for the big milestones to throw a party? Create mini celebrations for your small wins. Finished a big report at work? Treat yourself to your favorite coffee or snack. Finally completed that online course? Have a mini dance party in your living room. These small acts of celebration help reinforce the positive feelings associated with progress and make the journey toward your big goals more enjoyable.

The point isn't the size of the celebration—it's the act of acknowledging your effort. Celebrating even the smallest victories can give you a sense of accomplishment and keep you motivated for the next step.

3. Reward Yourself in Meaningful Ways

Rewards don't have to be grand gestures. In fact, small, meaningful rewards can be just as motivating. After achieving a small win, give yourself a reward that aligns with your values or brings you joy. Maybe it's taking a break to read a chapter of a book, treating yourself to a delicious meal, or indulging in a relaxing bath.

By associating your accomplishments with positive experiences, you reinforce the idea that progress, no matter how small, is worth celebrating. This builds positive habits and makes achieving your goals feel more like a journey you're enjoying rather than a mountain you have to climb.

4. Share Your Wins with Others

Celebrating small wins doesn't have to be a solo activity. Sharing your achievements with others can amplify the sense of accomplishment and bring a sense of community to your journey. Whether it's with close friends, family, or even online communities, letting others in on your progress can make it feel even more rewarding.

The next time you achieve a small win—whether it's finishing a workout challenge or making progress on a project—share it with someone who will celebrate with you. Not only does this create an opportunity to bond over shared victories, but it also helps to build accountability and support along the way.

5. Visualize Your Progress

One of the most satisfying ways to celebrate small wins is to see your progress visually. Create a progress board, where you can track each step of your journey. Whether it's a fitness goal, a financial target, or a personal project, seeing your progress in real-time can be incredibly motivating.

You can use a traditional chart or a more creative approach, like adding stickers or color-coded notes to track each accomplishment. Watching your progress grow over time serves as a powerful reminder that small wins add up to big success.

Wrapping It Up: Making Every Win Count

Success isn't just about the big moments. It's about the little steps, the everyday efforts, and the small wins that get you there. By celebrating your progress along the way, you stay motivated, avoid burnout, and create a positive feedback loop that propels you forward.

So, go ahead—celebrate that finished to-do list, that morning workout, that one-page chapter you wrote today. No win is too small to acknowledge, and every win deserves recognition. After all, it's the small victories that lead to the big ones, and life is too short not to celebrate every step along the way.

Let's start making every day a celebration of progress—because, at the end of the day, those small wins are what keep us moving forward.

Allison T Garrett

CHAPTER EIGHTEEN

A Call to Action: Building a Resilient Future

As we near the end of this journey through resilience, success, failure, anxiety, and all the small wins in between, it's time to shift our focus outward. What does it mean to not only cultivate resilience in ourselves but to foster it in our families, communities, workplaces, and society as a whole? Building a resilient future requires a collective effort—one that embraces challenges, values growth, and redefines what it means to succeed in an ever-changing world.

In this chapter, we're issuing a call to action: to not only embody resilience in our own lives but to lead the charge in creating a culture that values resilience over perfection, adaptability over rigidity, and well-being over achievement at all costs.

The Need for a Resilient Culture

Let's face it: we live in a world that's increasingly defined by uncertainty, rapid change, and unpredictability. From global crises to personal struggles, we're constantly being challenged in ways that push us to our limits. In such a world, resilience isn't just a nice trait to have—it's essential for survival and thriving.

Yet, despite the importance of resilience, many aspects of our culture work against it. We're often encouraged to avoid discomfort, seek quick fixes, and expect immediate results. Social media amplifies unrealistic standards of success, while the constant rush of modern life leaves little room for reflection, recovery, or personal growth. As a result, many people feel overwhelmed, burned out, and disconnected from their own strength and potential.

What we need is a cultural shift—one that encourages people to face challenges head-on, embrace failure as a learning tool, and build strong support networks that help individuals bounce back from adversity. A resilient culture fosters growth, not perfection, and celebrates perseverance, not just success.

The Reality Check: The Impact of Resilience on Society

The benefits of fostering resilience go far beyond personal well-being. Resilient individuals contribute to stronger, more adaptable communities, organizations, and even economies. When people have the tools to navigate setbacks and recover from challenges, they are more likely to take risks, innovate, and collaborate—all essential ingredients for a thriving society.

Let's take a look at how resilience can transform several aspects of our world:

1. **Resilient Communities**: Communities that foster resilience are better equipped to handle crises, whether it's a natural disaster, economic downturn, or social unrest. These communities prioritize mutual support, adaptability, and shared responsibility, allowing them to respond to challenges with creativity and strength. Think of neighborhoods that come together after a hurricane to rebuild, or groups that organize mutual aid networks during a pandemic. These communities don't just survive—they emerge stronger.

2. **Resilient Workplaces**: In the professional world, resilience is key to innovation and long-term success. Companies that encourage their employees to take risks, learn from failure, and prioritize well-being over constant productivity create environments where creativity can thrive. Resilient workplaces are not just about hitting quarterly targets—they're about cultivating a culture where employees feel supported, engaged, and empowered to grow.

3. **Resilient Educational Systems**: Schools and universities that focus on resilience equip students with the skills they need to thrive in an ever-changing world. This means instructing students not just to memorize facts or pass exams, but to develop problem-solving skills, emotional intelligence, and the ability to adapt to new situations. Educational systems that emphasize resilience prepare students for real-world challenges, helping them navigate the difficulties of life with confidence.

4. **Resilient Economies**: Economies that prioritize resilience are better able to withstand shocks and recover from crises. This means supporting small businesses, encouraging innovation, and investing in social safety nets that help individuals and communities bounce back from economic setbacks. A resilient economy is one that values long-term sustainability over short-term gains and fosters a sense of shared responsibility for collective well-being.

Leading the Way to Resilience

So, how do we start building a more resilient culture? The good news is that resilience begins with individual actions, and those actions can ripple out to create broader change. Here are some fun and creative ways to lead the way in fostering resilience in your community, workplace, or even within your family.

1. Host Resilience-Building Workshops

One way to promote resilience in your community or workplace is by hosting workshops or events focused on resilience-building skills. These can range from mindfulness and stress management techniques to creative problem-solving exercises. Invite people to share their own experiences with overcoming challenges, and create a space for learning and growth.

Workshops don't have to be formal or stuffy—why not make them fun? Think "Resilience Bootcamp," where participants tackle mini challenges designed to push them out of their comfort zones in a supportive environment. By making resilience-building interactive and engaging, you'll inspire others to embrace the process.

2. Create a Resilience Accountability Group

Form a group with friends, colleagues, or community members where you regularly check in on each other's resilience goals. Maybe someone is working on becoming more adaptable at work, while another person is trying to bounce back from a personal setback. By creating a space for mutual support and accountability, you help each other stay motivated and resilient in the face of challenges.

The key here is to create an atmosphere of encouragement, not judgment. Celebrate small wins, share insights from failures, and remind each other that resilience is a practice, not a destination.

3. Celebrate Resilience Stories

Start a "Resilience Story" series in your community, workplace, or social circle. Invite people to share their own stories of overcoming adversity, learning from failure, or navigating tricky situations. These stories can be shared in newsletters, social media, or even through in-person events.

By highlighting real-life examples of resilience, you'll inspire others to see challenges as opportunities for growth. Plus, sharing stories helps normalize the idea that failure is part of the process and that bouncing back is a sign of strength, not weakness.

4. Incorporate Resilience Practices in Everyday Life

You don't need a grand platform to promote resilience—you can start right where you are, in your daily life. Model resilience by being open about your own struggles and how you've overcome them. Encourage your family, friends, or coworkers to practice self-care, take breaks, and seek support when they need it.

In your own life, focus on building daily habits that promote resilience. This could be setting aside time for mindfulness, journaling about your small wins, or practicing gratitude. When you prioritize your own well-being, you're better equipped to handle challenges—and you set an example for others to follow.

5. Advocate for Resilience-Focused Initiatives

On a larger scale, you can advocate for policies and programs that promote resilience in your community or workplace. This might include pushing for mental health resources at work, supporting local businesses that contribute to economic resilience, or getting involved in community projects that strengthen social connections.

Advocacy doesn't have to be daunting—it can start with a conversation. Talk to your employer about implementing resilience training, or work with local leaders to create programs that support vulnerable populations. By advocating for resilience on a larger scale, you help create systems that support long-term growth and adaptability.

Wrapping It Up: The Path to a Resilient Future

As we wrap up this chapter, let's take a moment to reflect on the bigger picture. Building a resilient future starts with each of us. By embracing resilience in our own lives and leading by example, we can create a culture that values growth, adaptability, and connection over perfection and rigid success.

We've covered a lot of ground in this book—overcoming fear, embracing failure, celebrating small wins, and adapting to change. But the ultimate goal is to carry these lessons forward, not just for ourselves, but for those around us. The future belongs to the resilient, and together, we can build a world where challenges are seen as opportunities, and growth is a lifelong journey.

So, consider this your call to action. Whether you're leading a resilience workshop, sharing your story of overcoming adversity, or simply taking time to celebrate your daily wins, you're contributing to a stronger, more resilient future. Let's rise to the challenge, embrace the journey, and create a world where resilience isn't just a buzzword—it's a way of life.

Allison T Garrett

FINAL THOUGHTS

Why This Matters (And Why It Should Matter to You, Too)

If you've made it this far, then you know by now that resilience isn't just a buzzword to me—it's the heartbeat of everything I believe in. It's what gets us through the darkest nights, the hardest days, and those moments when we feel like we just can't take another step. It's not about ignoring the challenges or pretending life is a walk in the park—it's about facing the hard shit head-on and coming out the other side stronger, more capable, and ready for whatever comes next.

But let me be clear: this isn't about dismissing mental health struggles. I've lived through trauma. My childhood was filled with moments that would have broken a lesser woman—or so I've been told. I dropped out of school to help my dad take care of my siblings when I lost my mother, and then I lost him just two years later. Trust me, I know what it feels like to be pushed to the brink. Trauma is real, and I don't want anyone to think I'm suggesting that trauma *alone* makes you resilient. It doesn't. Trauma can break you if you let it, and mental health conditions are serious—damn serious. I've worked with too many women who've been trapped in cycles of anxiety, depression, and self-doubt to take that lightly. This book isn't about dismissing those struggles, but about finding ways to break the cycle, to practice resilience, and to create a life that's not defined by fear or past pain.

So why focus on resilience? Because while trauma doesn't make you resilient, the choice to rise in the face of hardship does. That's the difference. I've seen women rise. I've seen them practice resilience in the everyday moments of life—whether that's juggling a demanding job and motherhood, dealing with the breakdown of a marriage, or struggling to make ends meet. And here's the kicker: every time we practice resilience, we're not just doing it for ourselves. We're doing it for our children.

Look, I mostly work with women. My heart has always been for the women who are carrying the weight of the world on their shoulders, and often, they don't even realize how strong they are. But this book? It's just as much about children as it is about us. Why? Because these kids we're raising today—they are our future. They are the ones who will inherit this world and, frankly, they'll be the ones caring for us when we're old and gray (or maybe fabulously silver-haired). So, let's get real—how we equip our children matters. Big time.

When women—mothers, aunts, teachers, role models—begin to acknowledge their areas of opportunity to practice resilience, they not only transform their own lives but also create a ripple effect that touches the next generation. By modeling resilience in our everyday lives, we teach our children that it's okay to struggle, to fail, and to get back up again. We show them that life isn't about avoiding discomfort but about facing it with grit and grace.

It's easy to get caught up in the "old school versus new school" debate when it comes to parenting and resilience. My upbringing was definitely old school—I didn't have the luxury of helicopter parents or "safe spaces." But that doesn't mean I'm here to tell you we need to toughen up our kids by throwing them into the deep end of life without a life vest. What I'm saying is, there's a balance. There's a middle ground where we can acknowledge mental health, support our kids' emotional needs, and still teach them the value of resilience.

Because the truth is, resilient children become resilient adults, and resilient adults build stronger communities. And isn't that the goal? To raise a generation that can handle life's challenges with confidence, to stop the cycle of fragility and helplessness, and to empower our children to stand on their own two feet when the storms of life inevitably come?

I want this book to challenge you to think differently. To reflect on how you show up in your own life and how that influences the children around you. Are you practicing resilience, or are you avoiding discomfort? Are you teaching your kids to face challenges head-on, or are you sheltering them from every bump in the road? Trust me, the little eyes watching you—whether they're your own kids, nieces, and nephews, or even your neighbor's kid—they're taking notes. They're learning how to navigate life based on what *you* do, not what you say.

The stakes are high. These kids will one day be the leaders, the caregivers, the ones holding the world together. And here's the truth: they need us to show them the way. They need us to teach them that resilience isn't just about getting through the tough times—it's about growing from them.

So, here's my final call to action: start with yourself. Take a good, hard look at how you're practicing resilience in your own life. Where are your opportunities to grow? How can you stop letting fear, anxiety, or old habits hold you back? And how can you start modeling resilience for the kids who will one day inherit the world we're shaping today?

It's not about being perfect. Hell, I've stumbled more times than I can count. But it's about showing up, doing the work, and teaching the next generation to do the same. Because in the end, it's not about the traumas we face—it's about what we do with them. It's about creating a future where our kids can stand strong, not because life was easy, but because they were taught how to rise after every fall.

Now let's go build that future—one resilient child, one resilient community, one resilient generation at a time.

SELF-REFLECTION

Identifying Personal Resilience

1. **When was the last time I faced a significant challenge? How did I respond, and what strengths did I rely on to get through it?**
   - Reflect on a recent tough situation and identify the qualities that helped you persevere. Was it your problem-solving skills, your determination, or maybe your ability to seek help?

2. **What are three things I've overcome in my life that I never thought I could?**
   - List some of the hardest experiences you've faced. How did these experiences shape you, and what did they teach you about your resilience?

3. **In moments of stress or failure, what are the thoughts I tend to have? Do they build me up or tear me down?**
   - Take an honest look at your internal dialogue. Is it critical, encouraging, or somewhere in between? How could you reframe negative self-talk to strengthen your resilience?

4. **When life gets tough, what are the habits or coping mechanisms I turn to? Are they healthy and supportive, or do they need improvement?**
   - Consider whether your current ways of handling stress are helping or hindering your growth. Are there more positive habits you could adopt?

5. **How do I handle failure? Do I see it as a learning opportunity, or do I tend to dwell on it?**
   - Reflect on how you perceive failure. How can you shift your mindset to see setbacks as stepping stones for growth rather than personal shortcomings?

Parenting: Modeling and Raising Resilience

6. **How do I currently react when my children face challenges? Do I step in immediately, or do I allow them to figure things out on their own?**
   - Think about your default parenting style. Are you more of a "fixer," or do you give your children space to navigate obstacles? How might your approach influence their ability to be resilient?

7. **What messages do I consciously or unconsciously send my children about failure and mistakes?**
   - Reflect on how you talk about failure in your household. Do you encourage risk-taking and growth, or is there a fear of getting things wrong? How could you shift the narrative around mistakes?

8. **What are some small challenges I can allow my children to face on their own, even if it's uncomfortable for me to watch?**
   - Identify areas where you might step back and let your children struggle a bit to build their own resilience. How can you support them while giving them room to grow?

9. **When was the last time I shared a personal story of resilience with my children? How can I use my own experiences to teach them about overcoming adversity?**
    - Consider whether you're open about your own struggles and triumphs with your kids. How can sharing your stories help them see that everyone faces challenges and that resilience is built over time?

10. **In what ways can I encourage my children to take healthy risks and face challenges, rather than shielding them from failure?**
    - Think about how you can foster a growth mindset in your kids. What opportunities can you create for them to step out of their comfort zones and build resilience through small, everyday risks?

Practical Resilience in Daily Life

11. **How do I handle everyday stress (work, family, responsibilities)? What is one small change I can make to improve my response to daily pressures?**
    - Identify one practical area of life—whether it's balancing work or managing household duties—where you could improve your resilience. Maybe it's setting better boundaries or practicing mindfulness.

12. **How can I create more moments in my day to reflect on small wins and progress, rather than waiting for big milestones?**
    - Consider how you can celebrate your small victories, whether it's through journaling, sharing with loved ones, or simply taking a moment to acknowledge your progress.

13. **Who are the people in my life that support my resilience, and who might undermine it? How can I cultivate relationships that strengthen my ability to bounce back?**
    - Reflect on the people around you. How do your relationships contribute to or detract from your resilience? What boundaries or changes might you need to implement?

14. **What's one habit I can introduce to my daily routine that helps build resilience—whether it's self-care, setting goals, or practicing gratitude?**
    - Identify one action you can take every day to fortify your mental and emotional strength. It could be something simple, like a morning gratitude practice or setting a small, achievable goal for the day.

15. **How can I be more intentional about modeling resilience for my children in the way I handle stress, failure, or disappointment?**
    - Think about how you can show your children resilience through your own actions. How can you demonstrate that it's okay to feel frustrated, but it's important to keep going? What habits or attitudes can you adopt to make resilience a visible part of your daily life?

Long-Term Vision for Raising Resilient Kids

16. **What kind of resilience skills do I hope my children will have when they become adults? What can I do now to help them develop those skills?**

    - Think about the long-term. What resilience-building experiences can you create for your kids today to ensure they grow into strong, adaptable adults?

17. **How can I balance supporting my children emotionally while also encouraging their independence and problem-solving skills?**

    - Consider how you can walk the line between being a nurturing parent and letting your children navigate their own challenges. What adjustments can you make to give them both emotional support and the space to grow?

18. **How can I create opportunities for my children to contribute to our family, community, or larger world in a way that builds their resilience?**

    - Explore ways to involve your kids in family responsibilities or community service. Giving them responsibilities that matter not only builds confidence but also shows them they can handle real-world challenges.

Legacy of Resilience

19. **How do I want to be remembered by my children and future generations in terms of how I faced challenges and modeled resilience?**
    - Picture your legacy. What kind of example do you want to set for your children when it comes to dealing with life's ups and downs? How can you start living that legacy now?

20. **What's one way I can begin practicing resilience today, and how can I share that lesson with my children?**
    - Think about a challenge you're facing today. How can you model resilience by tackling it head-on? How can you turn this into a teachable moment for your kids?

www.ingramcontent.com/pod-product-compliance
Lightning Source LLC
LaVergne TN
LVHW100146061126
851857LV00010B/260
* 9 7 9 8 2 1 8 6 0 7 9 6 8 *